THE Wine Avenger

WILLIE GLUCKSTERN

Illustrations by Ben Crumlich

A FIRESIDE BOOK/PUBLISHED BY SIMON & SCHUSTER

FIRESIDE
Rockefeller Center
1230 Avenue of the Americas
New York, NY 10020

DESIGNED BY JILL WEBER

Manufactured in the United States of America
10 9 8 7 6 5 4

Library of Congress Cataloging-in-Publication Data:
Gluckstern, Willie.
The wine avenger / Willie Gluckstern : illustrations by Ben Crumlich.
p.   cm.
"A Fireside book."
Includes index.
1. Wine and wine making. I. Title.
TP548.G53   1998
641.2'2—DC21   98-16869
CIP

ISBN 0-684-82257-1

For my great, good friend Nancy Maniscalco,
who gave me a wine shop to fill

Acknowledgments

I really, really, really, really want to thank:

My editor, Sarah Baker, who dreamt it up, conned me into pitching it, and forced me to finish the cockamamie thing. My assistant, Evan Spingarn, whose editing, organizational skills, and fine ear for clarity, wit, and censorship saved the day. And Ben Crumlich, ace taster, wine/food free thinker, and uncanny, mind-melding illustrator.

Special thanks to Chef Rocco DiSpirito, who—God bless him—got it; sommelier Urs Kaufmann; "Food Avenger" Steve Jenkins, Avatar of Fermented Milk; Rick Smilow and Chef Cathy Kaufman of Peter Kump's New York Cooking School, my wine/food laboratory; and Riesling's blessed College of Cardinals: importers Bob Rice, Terry Thiese, David Thompson, and Rudi Wiest.

Also thanks to Mark Hutchens, Susan Klingelhoffer, Megan Moynihan, and Steve Orloff.

Finally, thanks my late father, Steve Gluckstern, who started out selling whiskey in Chinatown in 1946, got the wine bug in the '50s, gave it to me in the '60s, and taught me two timeless wine business stratagems:

When you get something for nothing, you never get finished paying for it, and . . .

Don't let the door hit you in the ass on the way out.

Contents

Preface

Why another wine book? The subject of wine is incredibly complicated. Which is why all wine books are incredibly complicated. This one is simple. If you like, you may think of it as a sort of extended article in the food section of your daily newspaper . . . or simply the rantings of a bitter malcontent, legitimized by a major publisher who has lost touch with reality.

Why me? I have nothing to lose. I am beholden to no one in the wine industry. I am a nonlistener to wine talk and a nonbeliever of wine publicists, and I have zero interest in winery owners, winemakers, and their glad-handing gunsels. "Shut up and put it in the glass," I say. I'm difficult, I admit it. But it's the best way I've found to wade through oceans of mediocre wine in my search for pearls.

Why you? It's fun, it's easy, it's controversial, and it's cheap. What the hell?

Introduction

Most of us are not raised feeling comfortable with wine. The maturing American generally learns his first lesson in wine appreciation at sixteen, puking white Zinfandel in the high school parking lot. An atmosphere of easygoing wine enjoyment and experimentation as part of daily life is later stifled in uncertain consumers by a pernicious image of wine elitism. Feature stories in the media about millionaires' cellars, rare wine auctions, and chi-chi small production boutique wineries are prime culprits. The wine industry compounds the problem by shamelessly marketing a make-believe lifestyle that elevates mass-produced, mediocre wines to a naïve public that not only doesn't know any better but is too intimidated to even ask.

So the average Joe in the street has nearly zero useful knowledge of wine. He leads a busy life and has little time or interest for the subject. He figures one glass of wine is pretty much the same as the next. Plus, isn't really good wine expensive anyway? And as many wine writers and food critics cavalierly advise, "Whatever you like to drink is fine with whatever you're eating." Right? Wrong, all wrong.

Someone has to straighten Joe out. He needs a clear voice of reason to set him on the true path to vinous enlightenment—or at least to a decent glass of wine. Perhaps a Clive, a Serena, or a Jancis could serve. But Willie Gluckstern? Who the hell is that?

I started out working in liquor warehouses at night, picking orders and loading trucks. I later rode those liquor trucks delivering the stuff—even wine sometimes. Then I was a wine salesman for a lot of years, followed by restaurant consulting, writing wine lists, and training wait staffs. This I still do.

I have taught nearly a thousand wine classes in the past twenty-five years and attended two or three times that many trade tastings. I have become, by force of habit and necessity of speed, a good taster. Not a good taster in the way gazetteers like Robert Parker or Steven Tanzer are; I'm too busy making buying decisions for my clients to spend much time on the details of tasting—cooperage, pH, Brix, and all that techno stuff. Hell, truth be told, I haven't written a tasting note in fifteen years. Really top wines are so rare at every price point that simply finding one worth drinking is a small miracle.

Unfortunately, like so many others in the wine trade, I've become a bit jaded. So many wines, so little time, etc. But all this tasting and teaching has taught me how to reduce the subject to its practical essentials. For that I am grateful. It has simplified things for me, allowing me more time for my other passions: plants and music.

My aim here is to do the same for you, to free you up, to empower you, to upgrade all hell out of your wine program in under 200 pages. What's provided here is a kind of survival kit, only what you really need to know: *How to recognize a good wine and when to serve it.*

TASTE

It's Not What You Think

$\mathcal{B}$efore we can begin to judge a wine's quality, we must understand the tasting process. How do we taste? More to the point, where do we taste? The answer seems obvious, of course: in the mouth, on some magical, elusive "palate."

Sit down. You need to know something about your mouth. It doesn't really taste. The closest we can come to the traditional idea of tasting with the mouth is to understand its shared connection to the nose. We experience flavor in just one place—back behind the nasal cavity. This is where aroma *becomes* taste.

THE NOSE

The nose is the epicenter for all tasting experience, and understanding the way it works is fascinating.

The tasting launchpad is a tiny hingelike apparatus called the *olfactory epithelium*. There, just behind the nose, aromatic molecules are caught and interpreted by approximately 15 million receptors. Instantly, these receptors fire off impulses to the brain's olfactory cortex, which translates them into specific flavors.

There are two routes that aromas can take to reach the olfactory

epithelium: outside, via the nose, and from inside the mouth, through the interior nasal passages.

During normal breathing, only about 15 percent of the air we take in reaches the olfactory epithelium. When we nose a glass of wine or inhale strongly, we suck up far more air (and wine aromatics). This sniffing process is the first, highly revealing insight into a wine's flavor. Only a fool lifts a wineglass to his lips without first relishing its aroma.

Availing ourselves of even the most modest amateur tasting experience and scent memory, we soon learn to feel certain that we know just how a wine will taste from that very first scent. And we are most often right on target.

Second Scent: The Inside Route

It is when we bring wine inside the hothouse that is our mouth that true flavor is realized. Additional aromatics are made more volatile by the warmth of the mouth and by the wider surface area the wine is now exposed to. This is why tasters are forever swirling wine around in their wineglasses and in their mouths—to expose the wine to more air, thus releasing more aromatics. Once a wine completely coats the interior of the mouth, a far more powerful scent wafts up the *interior pathway,* where it delivers the definitive data to the olfactory epithelium. Remember as kids when you made one another laugh with milk in your mouths, and it came spraying out of your nose? That was fun, huh? Well, that milk reached your nose through the interior pathway, as does the critical second scent. Who knew?

THE MOUTH

You are right to ask at this point, "What the hell is the tongue used for anyway?" Calm down. In case you missed this in high school, there are four basic elements experienced by the tongue: acid, sugar, salt, and bitterness. Saltiness and bitterness, while useful in assessing the wider flavor range of foods, have little relevance to wine. So what's left is simply acid and sugar—the key elements in any wine's drinkability. And they are critical to the way a wine reacts with food.

But acid and sugar are experienced by degrees, not by what we call flavor—they are more experienced quantitatively than qualitatively. In fact, most of the surface area of the tongue has little sensitivity to flavors at all. But the tongue does react powerfully to the holy duo of acid and sugar.

The tip of the tongue tells your brain how sweet a wine is (not so

sweet or kind of sweet or very sweet or achingly sweet). The tongue's upper edges relay a wine's acidity (sort of flat, a little juicy, mouthwatering, rapierlike, or able to cut through steel). So the tongue doesn't really *taste,* it measures.

Taste, then, is the impact of a wine's *aromatics* on the olfactory epithelium, plus the tactile sensation of a wine's *mouthfeel.* Put simply, the $E = mc^2$ of taste is the melding of aroma and mouthfeel.

WINE AND FOOD
The Basics

Most people choose to ignore the possibility that any rhyme or reason might apply to matching wines with food. After all, choosing the right wine seems awfully complicated, and it doesn't matter much anyway. We drink what we like. If food arrives, so be it. I figure that's most people's take on the subject. But like it or not, profound chemical changes occur when wine meets food and both meet saliva. These changes alter the flavor of both, sometimes for the better but more often for the worse.

For years I've conducted wine/food workshops with people who are passionate about food but don't really understand how it connects with wine. These tastings are simple and objective. A chef prepares a seven-course menu, appetizer through dessert, the sort of things you might eat at home or in a restaurant. With each course, I serve four wines. We taste the wines by themselves, and then we taste the dish with each of the four wines. It's not very complicated, but the results are illuminating.

There are a handful of grape varieties that consistently outperform all others with food. Those winning varieties are not the ones you'd expect—or what you've probably been drinking. The absolute best white wine varieties for food are **Riesling, Chenin Blanc,** and **Sauvignon Blanc**. The food-friendliest red varieties are **Cabernet Franc, Gamay, Barbera,** and **Pinot Noir**.

Of course, there are many other grape varieties that also work well with food, but none as consistently or as flatteringly as those named above. In fact, it's shocking how most foods have their flavor ruined by Chardonnay, Cabernet, and Merlot, wines made from the world's three most popular grape varieties. If you drink wine simply as a social beverage, drink any damned thing you like. If food is an important part of your life, though, you should get to know the seven varieties mentioned above. But be prepared for a challenge. Because of the public's lemming-like devotion to Chardonnay, Cabernet, and Merlot, the market dictates that first-class examples of the best food wines will always be a challenge to track down. "Watson! The game is afoot!"

"FIRST, DO NO HARM"

Food amplifies everything in a wine. That means that lighter wines have more room to grow. They are actually fleshed out by their contact with food. On the other hand, Chardonnay, Cabernet, and Merlot—typically rich, heavyweight, high-alcohol wines that are even further pumped up by new oak (a ubiquitous sweetening agent)—tend to land on the diner's palate like an anvil. They are so massive and overpowering that they obliterate the flavor of all but the richest red meats and sauces. Little that we eat can stand up to these big, showy wines. In a very real sense, they *are* food.

Yes, even the famous châteaux wines of Bordeaux fall into this category. No matter how many overinflated scores, price increases, and fancy, shmancy auctions they beget, they still require a bloody slab of red meat or game to make sense at the table. Though often complex and seductive on their own or with French haute cuisine (their natural, indigenous partner, after all), they become bloated and unbalanced when paired with lighter dishes. Let's not even talk about what happens to the food. But if breaking the "Bordeaux with everything" fallacy isn't enough to rock your world, perhaps the greatest wine myth of all is that big, high-alcohol, oaked-to-kingdom-come American white wines are fit for food at all. American, Australian, and other "New World" wines made in this fashionable, mass-market style find themselves at a distinct disadvantage at the table. They simply choke on their own well-endowed attributes.

Night after night in restaurants across the country, exquisitely flavored white meat and fish dishes are laid waste by ludicrously priced, oak-thickened Chardonnays ordered more out of sheer bravado than anything else. The successful marriage of wine and food is best achieved when each complements the other. Wine should function as a support and enhancement to food, not a combatant. Sumptuous, over-the-top wines overpower delicate food flavors, leaving only the taste of the wine. We actually need to cleanse our palate with water or bread just so we can enjoy the food again!

Less Is More

Wine industry people—salesmen, retailers, and restaurateurs—are always going on about rich, chewy wines that can stand up to this and stand up to that. All this "standing up" sounds great when the boys are boasting, but how many artery-clogging feasts that can support these wines do people actually eat these days?

Which wine writer's or critic's ratings you cleave to is insignificant in the larger scheme of things. Ninety-point scores in wine magazines, feature stories, and county fair gold medals are a wonder to behold and certainly sell the bejeezus out of a wine, but they bear no relevance to how that wine will perform with food. Wine judges record their impressions in a neutral environment, sans food. We need to know how a wine drinks at the kitchen table, not in a sterile tasting room. No matter whether you pour yourself a glass of a 90-

point or an 86-point Cabernet Sauvignon with your pasta pomodoro, you still wind up with a train wreck in your mouth.

The most opulent power-packed wines represent the pinnacle of the winemaker's art, or so they say. I say there is just as much art in crafting an elegant, tautly balanced, medium-weight wine that fine-tunes the palate for subtle, complex food—and a finer art, at that.

MOUTHFEEL

A singularly important characteristic shared by all the best wines is their *balanced mouthfeel.* Just as aroma informs us of flavor, mouthfeel tells us nearly all we need to know about wine/food compatibility. It is the coming together of the tactiles (acid, sugar, alcohol, and weight) and is the most important consideration when it's time to dine.

Light to Medium Body

Since many of the foods that we actually eat here at ground zero—chicken breasts, salads, sandwiches, seafood, and pasta—are on the light side, our wines should be also.

Low Tannin

Tannins—primarily a feature of heavily extracted, age-worthy red wines—act as a firm counterpoint with red meats and other fatty or oily preparations (terrific with steak, lamb, duck, etc.). They are a mouth-drying, astringent bummer with nearly everything else, especially spicy food.

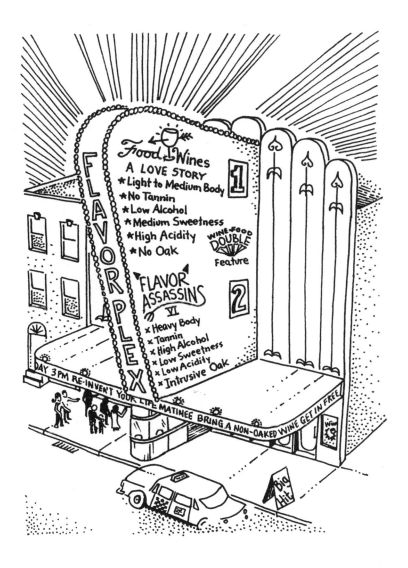

21

Low Alcohol

Food intensifies everything in wine, particularly alcohol, so an alcohol level over 12.5% had better be part of a well-balanced total package. Remember, if you can smell the alcohol or a wine feels hot in the mouth, the wine's a loser *with or without food.*

Medium Sweetness

Only sweeter wines, those with riper fruit qualities, can straddle both salty *and* sweet dishes. Why is this so important? Because few of us realize just how sweet most foods are.

There is almost no method of food preparation, save steaming or boiling, that does not *add* sweetness. The essence of browning is, by definition, *caramelization.* Caramelization occurs in nearly everything that hits the pan, the grill, or even the toaster. Your morning toast is comforting and mouthwatering at six o'clock, not simply because it's crisp and warm but because browning has made it sweet. Fry an onion, grill a salmon steak, or throw a shrimp on the barbie, and you need comparable sweetness in your wine. In fact, a medium degree of sweetness is nearly always welcome with food. The highbrow concept of a *dry* wine always being a more sophisticated choice is naïve at best.

High Acidity

Mouthwatering acidity is the indispensable key to any wine's food compatibility. Acid creates saliva, and saliva breaks down both food and wine in the mouth, releasing complex flavors. Hence, no acid, no taste. Acidity also provides refreshment. Think about that glass of fresh orange juice next to your morning toast, and its lively, awakening effect on your mouth. A first-class white wine is not a "mellow" wine. It should be a wake-up call anytime of the day.

No Oak

Oak is a taste distraction. It creates a woody, saccharine coating in the mouth that cuts off a wine's flavor as it imposes its own. Wine critics often note and winemakers boast of the origin of the oak barrels used in certain wines (French Limousin, Nevers, Troncais, etc.). No matter what forest the oak grew in, its texture and flavor are often overpowering at the table in red wines, and anathema in whites. If you are actually capable of identifying a specific sub-species of tree in your wineglass, you really need to get out more often.

8th Century
Legends
Part I

St. Crispness slays
the mighty Toastbreath

WHERE DO GREAT WINES COME FROM?

Great wines don't grow on trees. If you assume that most wines are of good to excellent quality, then, my friend, you are living in a fool's paradise. The wine industry and its minions would like you to believe that nearly all wine is well made and delicious. The truth is very different.

The overwhelming majority of wine in the marketplace is mediocre at best. Country of origin makes no difference: Every winemaking nation on earth makes oceans of indifferent-to-execrable wine. Price matters not; there are as many lousy $40 bottles as $3.99 bottles. Brand names make no difference: After all, wineries whose ads appear in magazines and on the sides of buses must cleave to the ad industry maxim that there's no point in advertising nationally unless you have a nearly inexhaustible supply. It's safe to say that wines made in mass-market quantities usually taste that way.

In my work I taste thousands of wines each year, and I can tell you that at every price point—that's *every* price point—out of fifty wines tasted, I'll find only one or two genuine successes. That's not to say you'll need to have an ambulance idling outside the door when you open one of those forty-nine also-rans, but these wines are probably best described as common, unexciting, or just plain boring.

So why are really excellent wines so difficult to find? Would you believe . . . real estate? The most important influence on a wine's quality, as well as its price, is geography.

LOCATION, LOCATION, LOCATION

First-class grapes are very fussy about where they are cultivated. Unlike apples or lettuces, wine grapes achieve greatness only in well-drained soils of specific geological compositions in vineyards with steeply angled slopes that best capture the sun's nurturing rays. Soil and a vineyard's environs, or what the French call *terroir,* go a long way toward answering one of the most commonly asked wine questions: Why is a particular wine absolutely delicious, while a similarly priced wine, even one made from the same grape, is disappointing?

WEATHER

Throughout the better wine-growing areas of the world, there exist countless "microclimates." These tiny pockets of weather ultimately exert a powerful influence on fruit quality and explain why one winemaker's vineyard consistently enjoys near-perfect weather while his neighbor gets only hail. So, like retail on Broadway, it's essential to do business on the good side of the street.

VINES

When wine vines are young—say, under twenty-five years old— they produce good quality and copious quantity. Winery owners like this a lot—good juice and lots of it. But as a vine begins to age its way past thirty or thirty-five years, it produces fewer grapes.

Quality, however, gets finer and finer throughout the life of the vine plant, which can reach a gnarled old age of eighty years or more. So a vine continues to produce better wine as it ages but less of it. Bottom-line wineries (often run by corporations and other greedy bastards) routinely tear out thirty- and forty-year-old vines just as they are entering their best years. These producers lust for the most possible juice per plant. Period. One of the reasons that the fine, artisanal wines of the world are so rare and so much more expensive is that older vines are allowed and even encouraged to remain productive in the vineyard, resulting in somewhat reduced though superior-quality yields. In the mouth, wines made from old vines (*vieilles vignes*) can exert a special allure, a kind of sexy silkiness. They are usually worth the extra money. On the other hand, "old vines" on the label is no guarantee of quality. After all, it doesn't matter how ancient the vines are if they are stuck in a poorly situated vineyard. In most cases, *"vieilles vignes"* on a wine label really means *"raise ze price."* To be honest, most truly great wines contain a significant amount of juice from older vines without mentioning them on the label. They don't need to.

PRUNING

Hard pruning, or clipping away potential fruit, is an effective technique for limiting production and thus positively influencing quality. Even if a vine is young, less fruit is always better. If you garden, you know that when you prune away half of those pretty strawberry blossoms, the ones that go on to become fruit will be plumper and sweeter. It's worth the sacrifice.

With wine vines, this "close cropping" is critical to quality winemaking. This is why it's often said that a great wine is created in the vineyard, not in the winery. Vines that are allowed to overpro-

Soil (Terroir)

Climate

Older Vines

Hard Pruning

Heavy Spitting

Voilà

duce, as in most of the world's mass-market wines, result in thin, vapid *vin ordinaire* that is routinely dressed up and promoted with romantic labels and catchy names.

TALENT

Finally, there is the skill of the winemaker. A first-class winemaker can craft a palatable wine using less than fully ripe grapes, while a poor winemaker can take the world's ripest, most perfect grapes and turn out Pine-Sol.

A truly talented winemaker knows how to evaluate a given vintage's fruit as it comes into the winery, and how to allow it, with only gentle prodding, to *make itself* into wine. When fruit comes from a great vineyard site, the best winemakers do little but nurture. In other words, the less human intervention, the better. A bottle of wine is not made by a recipe, nor is it a painting requiring a winemaker's signature.

QUALITY
What to Look For

AROMA

*A*roma is *the* most accurate indicator of a wine's quality. And as we have seen, aroma is actually the very essence of what we call taste. Trust your nose! If it smells lousy, it is lousy. If you were to line up any group of thin, poorly made wines, their most obvious common flaw would be a lack of clean, fresh aromas.

Occasionally, a wine's aroma is so unusual that you may mistake its oddness for a flaw. If you have yet to experience a wide variety of wines, be patient. Some grapes display powerful aromatic signatures that may stun or mystify your senses. The intense lychee and rose petal scent of Alsace Gewürztraminer is a good example. Keep an open mind. At times these exotic smells can foretell quite a seismic taste experience (in a nice way, I mean).

Generally, the aroma of a well-made wine should be clean, attractive (whatever that means to you), and most important, faithfully characteristic of the wine's grape variety. For instance, when you've learned with some little tasting experience what Pinot Noir should smell like, you'll always know what to look for. Unfortunately, subtle, complex varieties like Pinot often have their delicacy marred or buried by too much contact with new oak or by other winemaking screwups.

COMPLEXITY:
"What the Hell Are They Smelling in There?"

When tasters wax rhapsodic about a wine's aroma growing more complex *(evolving)* in the glass because of aeration, what has often happened is that they've sniffed and inhaled the same scent over and over, acclimating the membranes of their olfactory cortex to the most prominent smell, or the wine's *primary aroma.* Now, more subtle aromas begin to emerge from the background. In other words, those oh-so-elusive *complexities* were there all along but were masked by the more dominant, primary aroma. For instance, the initial aromatic wallop of new oak and black currants in a top Bordeaux will fade after some minutes of *nosing* to reveal herb, tobacco, or even pencil lead.

How complex can wine become? Aromatic variations are nearly limitless, ranging from nectar-dripping orchids in a Tahitian paradise to the feral stink of a sun-warmed manure pile; from the sweet breath of newborn infants to the powdery smell at the bottom of an old lady's pocketbook. What's most fascinating is the incredible sensitivity of the human nose. According to the experts, hydrogen sulfide, the rotten-egg smell, can be detected by the average human in concentrations of just three parts per billion. This anytime-of-the-day miracle is the equivalent of locating a single family of three in China. Can you imagine what your dog's nose is capable of?

So to find levels of complexity in a wine, keep sniffing beyond the thirty seconds or several minutes it may take for your nose to "damp down" the wine's major scent. Most better wines will exhibit additional aromatic complexities with persistent nosing, but don't expect the spice galleons of old Cathay from every wine you meet.

FLAVOR

Flavor, ironically, is not all that important to the understanding or assessment of a wine's quality. While factors such as acid-sugar balance and aromatic intensity are virtually quantifiable, flavor is entirely subjective. Its appreciation is based on individual palate history, acquired taste, and of course, personal perception. What's more, nobody is going to enjoy every taste (ever tried Vegemite?). But the human palate is a wonder of complexity and possibility. And it evolves as it matures.

The grape varieties that go into the production of wine are as varied in flavor as are all the world's myriad varieties of fruit. Grapes in their liquid form become a cipher for endless flavor combinations, often resembling anything but grapes—for instance, Sauvignon Blanc (herbaceousness), Chablis (gunflint), Cabernet Franc (bell pepper), and American white wine (sawdust).

While flavor is certainly one determining factor in a wine's quality, it is far from the most important, especially when it comes to food, as we shall soon see.

BALANCE: THE TACTILES

We envision flavor as a simple one-note tune. But in ascertaining flavor, our mouths must instantaneously interpret an entire symphony of impressions. If the mouth is the musical instrument in this analogy, the musical parts it must read are chiefly acid and sugar. And like musicians, who have their own highly descriptive language for things, we wine people call this ensemble *mouthfeel*.

Acid

The first duty of a wine is to be juicy! Think of crisp apples or ripe peaches and the way they make your mouth water. A high-quality wine should have roughly the same effect. Acidity, a primary component in all wine grapes, is the source of wine's juiciness. Without it, a wine is boring to drink and useless at the table. This is especially true of sparkling and white wines, both sweet and dry, but is also of critical importance with reds. Wine without acidity is like some dead thing. *Morte.*

Crisp acids bring life and personality to wines. They make them interesting and exciting to drink, and they are the single distinguishing element that elevates real wine above the pop, faux wines of the masses. Acidity cannot be successfully integrated into a wine in the laboratory or at the winery. It must occur naturally in the vineyard.

How, then, can a wine achieve clean, crisp, natural acidity? And where do high-acid wines come from anyway? Sweetness can be achieved nearly anywhere grapes are grown if the sun performs well (warm climates) or if grapes are able to hang on the vine long enough (cool climates), but wines that consistently exhibit heightened levels of acidity are those made only from grapes grown in cool climates. You see, hot weather tends to burn off acidity, which is why grapes grown in regions where they can just barely ripen produce the juiciest wines.

If you lay out a map of the world and begin to check off the best white wine vineyards, you'll soon notice a common set of latitudes, sort of a wavelike thread that encircles the globe. This is why coolish wine regions such as Germany's Mosel; northern France's Alsace, Champagne, Chablis, and Loire regions; New Zealand's South Island; and even New York's Finger Lakes provide the best climate for the type of ripening scenario that creates the sharp crack of acidity that makes foodies salivate and wine geeks gawk.

Sometimes winemakers intentionally lower acidity in certain wines in order to refashion them in a softer, more "easy-drinking" style. Welcome to American white wine.

Malo What?

The most popular white wines made in America—Chardonnays and Sauvignon Blancs—usually have their acidity (what there is of it) further muted in order to appeal to the wine-shy American palate. There is a name for the winemaking process that accomplishes this; it's called *malolactic fermentation.* Stay with me, now. The next time you hear some wine geek or general know-it-all nonchalantly mention that such-and-such Chardonnay went through "a complete malolactic," you won't feel like such a backwoods boob for not knowing what the hell they're talking about.

There are two types of acids that pertain to grapes and the wines that are made from them: rapier-like malics (like the acid in apples) and softer lactics (like the acid in milk). Nearly all American winemakers encourage their white wines to undergo a second fermentation, one that converts the malics (juicy) into lactics (less juicy). This is the infamous malolactic fermentation, fabled in story and song, which when performed in unison with the traditional *sarabande de quercus* (sexy dancing with oak chips) makes all American white wines taste virtually the same and is the chief reason why flabby, oak-sweetened American whites perform so abysmally with food.

Sweetness

Most people erroneously believe that there are just two kinds of wine in the world—dry wines and sweet wines. They tend to equate the word sweet with sticky, sugared wines beloved by winos, high school miscreants, and your grandparents at the Jewish holidays. Dry wines, they reason, must be where the action is.

Entry-level wine consumers are renowned for naïvely flaunting their ignorance by asking for "a nice dry wine," a sure sign to wineshop clerks and waiters everywhere that these green consumers are sheep begging to be shorn.

MORE SUGAR!

The sugars that are created in fruits and vegetables ultimately influence the tastiness of those fruits and vegetables. Sugars, you see, amplify aromatics. The more sugars, the more aromatics. The more aromatics, the more flavor! Imagine corn-on-the-cob without its sweetness. Just chew on an ear that's been off the stalk a few days and has had its sugars converted to starch. It's tasteless.

Sarabande de Quercus

When it comes to wine, as in all matters of taste, the subtlety of language speaks volumes. If I say, "This wine has lovely sweet-ness," it is very different from saying, "This wine is sweet." The operative term here—and it's extremely important to be aware of—is sweet-*ness*. *Sweetness* in this context is not meant to describe a *dessert-grade* wine but rather to highlight the natural sweetness that results from the harvesting of magnificently ripe fruit, no mean feat in the world of winemaking. I do not refer to the vanilla bean sweetness leached from new oak barrels or oak chips but rather the delightful sensation of real sweetness, like that of a ripe berry, that we experience at the front of the mouth. That's why wine lovers become animated when they encounter sweetness in wines. They crave it in nearly everything but Champagne and Sauvignon Blanc, and that includes red wines like Cabernet, Mer-lot, and Pinot Noir. This *sweetness* does not stand alone and apart. It is an integral ingredient in a wine's overall makeup. It's not sim-ply how much sweetness a wine contains that speaks to its quality but how that sweetness is counterbalanced by the wine's acidity as well. Even the world's most unctuously sweet dessert wines achieve their greatness only when balanced by crisp, refreshing acidity.

A moderate degree of sweetness folded into a wine's overall pro-file is the winning formula for a wine that's perfect both for sipping by itself and for dining. This, of course, is not meant to belittle the importance of first-class wines that contain little or no residual sugar but merely to point out that fruitier wines enjoy a far greater variety of successful uses.

Mouthfeel

We've seen how we both smell and taste with our olfactory appa-ratus to ascertain a wine's quality, and how we judge a wine's degree of sweetness and acidity with the front part and the upper sides of our tongue. Another important part of quality assess-

ment involves tactility, or how a wine *feels* in the mouth. The term that best pinpoints this part of the tasting process is *mouthfeel,* or *body.* In this regard we ask, "How viscous is a wine? Is it light and delicate, rich and powerful, or somewhere in between? Does it make our mouths pucker up? Is it velvety? Chewy? Gritty? Does it feel like sandpaper?"

The elements that constitute mouthfeel are acid and sugar, extract (dry fruit solids), weight, alcohol, and tannin. We know all about acid and sugar now. Let's have a peek at the others.

EXTRACT

Extract is essentially a measure of what remains of a wine grape after you remove its water, or how much pure fruit concentrate exists. *Extract* is a winemaker's somewhat technical term, so let's cut to the chase and just call it the wine's *fruit,* as in "This wine has terrific fruit" or "Where's the bloody fruit?"

WEIGHT

Most red and white wines are considered medium-weight wines. Very dry whites and most rosés tend to be lighter in weight, while over-the-top reds, rich dessert wines, and ports are heavier in weight. The term *body* can be substituted for that of *weight*.

ALCOHOL

Alcohol occurs in all fermented beverages, whether it's beer (fermented grain), cider (fermented apples), mead (fermented honey), or wine (fermented grapes). In each case, yeast converts sugar into alcohol. The more sugar in the fermenting juice, the more alcohol you wind up with. While the percentage of alcohol in wine does vary greatly, we generally find them falling between 11 and 14%, though there are exceptions. In Germany, 9%, 8%, and even 7% alcohol levels are common, because of the briefer fermentation and the inherent qualities of Germany's indigenous grape varieties. Fresh, peachy Moscato d'Asti from Italy's Piedmont floats in at a delightfully low 5.5% alcohol, while thick, late-harvested Amarone from the Veneto routinely clocks in at a whopping 14.5%. Port wine reaches 19 or 20%, but it is actually fortified with a dash of brandy in order to stop the fermentation from consuming too much of the wine's glorious sweetness.

Alcohol content has a major influence on a wine's weight: The more alcohol, the richer the wine feels in the mouth. While more alcohol may sound like a positive thing, in most instances the reverse is true. The most frequent problems I encounter in evaluating wines are alcohol-related (in the wine, that is). Unless a wine has the requisite richness of fruit, too much alcohol can ruin an otherwise elegant wine. My rule is "If you can smell the alcohol, there's too much of it." If you can feel the burn of alcohol in the mouth, again there's too much of it. Even a wine with a reasonable level like 12.5% can taste hot if it lacks enough fruit to cushion its alcohol. All wines with too much alcohol should be considered flawed and are rarely pleasurable to drink. Not surprisingly, wines with less alcohol invariably fare better with most food.

That said, it is worth knowing that even a tiny increase in a wine's alcohol can have a significant physical effect on the wine drinker. The difference of a mere point and a half of alcohol between, say, a bottle at 12% and one at 13.5% shared between two diners can mean the difference between thanking the waiter, paying the check, and hailing a cab, or bumping into the waiter, knocking over the ice bucket, and falling off the curb into oncoming traffic.

Another typical scenario finds a pair of city dwellers at the end of a hard day's work cracking a bottle of California Chardonnay (13.5%, for sure) as they kick around which restaurant they'll head off to. By the time they're into their second glass, it's no surprise when one gives up and says, "Uh, why don't we just order in?" After all, they're nearly drunk by now, and that couch is starting to feel mighty comfy.

Now take the same pair, same situation, but substitute a 9% Mosel Riesling for the Chardonnay. They'll probably have finished their two glasses and be considering opening just one more before they go. Lower alcohol is good.

COLOR AND TANNIN IN RED WINES

What makes red wine red? Red wines, as opposed to white wines, are fermented *with* their skins, thereby extracting color pigments and tannins. All grape juice is essentially colorless, or white. When grape skins remain in contact with fermenting juice, that juice takes on the dark color of red wine. Hence, the skins of red wine grapes are separated out of fermenting Pinot Noir juice to create Champagne or Zinfandel juice to create the ubiquitous White Zinfandel.

Tannins are invisible, astringent compounds present in the skins, seeds, and stems of grapes. They create a drying sensation on the teeth, gums, and lips, sort of an exaggerated version of what your mouth feels like after sipping a cup of oversteeped black tea. Extremely tannic wines actually create an unpleasant, leather-like dryness in the mouth. These wines need fatty foils, like cheese and red meats, in order to soften their rough, tannic mouthfeel.

Red wine grapes that are notorious for producing tannic wines—like Bordeaux (Cabernet Sauvignon), Barolo (Nebbiolo), and Madiran (Tannat)—can evolve into some of the world's most fascinating red wines. This achievement is to a large degree the result of long-term bottle aging. Tannins from grape skins function as the support vehicle for this aging process. They become an integral part of the wine by remaining in the fermentation vessel in the grape skins for an extended period of time, say eight or ten days. This is known as extended skin contact, and assuming a red wine has lots of swell balance and extract to start with, it may mature for as long as twenty or thirty years or more, ultimately resulting in some sublimely nuanced nectar, though more often merely grist for high-profile wine auctions.

When tannic wines are young—in their first four or five years, say—they can be nearly undrinkable with all but the richest foods. As they continue to age, their tannins chemically link up with color pigments and begin to precipitate out as *sediment,* ultimately leaving the wine smooth, with hardly any trace of the gritty little devils.

The presence of significant tannin in rich, well-balanced, age-able red wines is definitely a positive attribute. These wines, though, represent a tiny portion of the general wine market. With the overwhelming majority of red wines, hard, gritty tannins are rarely present, as most reds are vinted to be consumed within three to five years of production.

FINISH OR LENGTH OF FLAVOR

Finish, simply put, is the integrity of flavor that remains after tasting a wine and noting the length of time it lingers. Five seconds or less is the typical short finish of a weak wine. Ten seconds or more is better. A minute or two is much better. An hour or more—see a doctor.

OAK

The MSG of Wine

Recipe for Chardonnay

One 10,000-gallon fermentation tank

10,000 gallons of Chardonnay grape juice

*Two 25-pound burlap sacks of oak chips
(extra-light, light, medium toast, extra-medium
toast, heavy toast, or extra-heavy toast)*

1. Toss oak sacks into tank with Chardonnay juice.
2. Let steep for about a month, lifting and dunking occasionally (like giant tea bags).
3. Fish out sacks.
4. Bottle and label.

Serves 106,000

Many kinds of containers are used to ferment grape juice into wine. The following are the three most popular:

1. **Stainless steel,** a neutral environment. It imparts nothing to the fermenting wine—zero aroma, flavor, or mouthfeel.
2. **Used oak** (barrels that have held wine in a previous year). It imparts weight and a rich, viscous mouthfeel without adding sweetness or flavoring.
3. **New oak.** It adds a lot: enriched body, tannin, and certain unmistakable aromas and tastes. These include vanilla, caramel, buttered toast, and all too often, burnt popcorn kernels. Above all, new oak adds its own nonvinous, rough-hewn sweetness.

WHAT OAK DOES

◆ The staves of oak barrels allow mild, beneficial oxidation of wines as they age.

◆ Oak enriches a wine's body and adds viscosity.

◆ Oak's natural tannins act as a preservative for wine (important for aging big reds and a few whites).

◆ It creates a vanilla-like sweetness.

Oak is generally used in the form of barrels. Wines *fermented* in oak barrels are far more powerfully influenced by its character than wines merely aged in them. Oak should be applied only to a wine that already boasts substantial weight and flavor of its own, and that means rich reds, primarily. While the expert use of oak barrels in the maturation of great *red* wines is essential, misuse merely contributes strong barrel flavors that obliterate any varietal aromas in a wine. Very few white wine varieties reap any benefit from contact with new oak. New oak acts on white wine like MSG, sweetening up but dumbing down whatever vibrant varietal signature exists.

For Chardonnay, the grape on which new oak cooperage is most often lavished, varietal character is a nonissue. As a variety, Chardonnay has so little flavor of its own that it is often entirely dependent on a winemaker's "recipe." Most Chardonnays are *created* in the winery with oak, not in the vineyard with pruning shears. For Riesling, Chenin Blanc, and Sauvignon Blanc, the food world's three most important white wine grape varieties, new oak is the Antichrist. The joy of these varieties as food mates is their freshness, delicacy, and succulence, all qualities that wilt in the presence of new wood.

THE OAKING OF AMERICA

For many years, the American public, who are by no definition daily wine drinkers, have been seduced by wines oaked in the most heavy-handed method imaginable. Virtually all under-$10 white wines produced in the United States are sugared with oak chips, powders, and essences. Oak-obsessed California winemakers simply will not let the poor palate-dead American consumer come up for air. (To be fair, neither will the Australians, South Africans, or Chileans.) It's nearly impossible to find a nonoaked domestic white wine of any kind, save a handful of East Coast whites and a very few West Coast examples (Randall Grahm's Malvasian bonbons). This begs the question: Why is virtually all white wine made in America bludgeoned with oak?

American wine drinkers, as well as those of countless other nations, are weaned on cold sweet drinks—fruit juice, soda pop, etc. Since all alcohol is puritanically forbidden here until at least voting age, we have never been a wine-drinking nation. Our first tentative contact with the grape is logically made most painless with a beverage of comparable sweetness to fruit juice and soda pop. Once we are initiated into a world of oaked wines, our reprogramming requires a complete reinterpretation of individual taste.

There are actually grape varieties that provide us with the sort of sweetness we love without relying on enhancement by nonliving substances. Unfortunately (or fortunately), these wondrous varieties don't flourish well in most parts of the world.

To satisfy the great American sweet tooth, the wine industry has marked each decade with a new "pop wine": Cold Duck in the sixties, Lambrusco in the seventies, white Zinfandel in the eighties, and finally in the nineties, the great seducer—Chardonnay.

Since Americans historically have little or no contact with clean, well-made, nonoaked wines, they neither understand nor enjoy them. They do enjoy the concept of wine—as long as it doesn't *taste* like wine. Oaked wines are far easier for non-wine-drinkers to deal with. They are mild, low-acid, sweet beverages that are popular for many of the same reasons as fast-food hamburgers: The taste is reliable, always the same—not great but no surprises.

The wine establishment, because of a combination of taking the path of least resistance and its own nonenlightened wine experience, has become an unwitting accomplice to this oak-driven madness.

When consumers, retailers, and restaurateurs cease associating the aroma of oak with quality, perhaps winemakers will stop abusing it. In my twenty-five years' experience teaching consumer and wait staff wine classes, I've found that when someone who's genuinely interested in wine tastes a range of examples uninfluenced by new-oak treatment, set out side by side with oaked wines, they become instant converts to "the real thing."

THE GRAPES

Of all the wine information you have absorbed before or during the reading of this book, no single element in the study of wine is more important than knowing your grapes. The flavor and aromatic characteristics of wines are determined first and foremost by the inherent genetic makeup of the grapes from which they are made. In other words, all grapes are *not* created equal. Geography, climate, and winemaking skills all play a part, but the ultimate quality of a given wine is limited to the potential of its grape variety.

Where food is concerned—and one must accept the premise of wine and food together as paramount—lighter, fruitier, more acidic wines (usually whites) are better. Heavier, higher-alcohol, oaky wines (usually reds) are far less versatile. In short, white wines go better with more foods than red wines. And what's more, you might say that the best red wines for most foods—the lighter, fruitier, and more acidic ones—are those that behave the most like whites.

Here, then, are my favorite food-friendly wine grapes:

WHITE	RED
Riesling	Cabernet Franc
Chenin Blanc	Barbera
Sauvignon Blanc	Gamay
	Pinot Noir

The following section defines each of these grapes in three ways: their overall character, where they are grown, and how they relate to food. Included as well are a dozen or so other grapes that are popular or otherwise relevant. Still others will be referred to in the chapters on wine and food pairings. For a more comprehensive listing of wine grapes, consult any other wine book.

Whites

CHARDONNAY

Chardonnay, the world's most overrated grape, has only fair acidity, negligible sweetness, and little flavor or aroma of its own. As a wine, the only things Chardonnay has a lot of—too much of—are alcohol and new oak.

Wildly popular in all its incarnations, Chardonnay is the standard bearer of the current "international style" of winemaking.

Its popularity with consumers is based on:

◆ its soft, unchallenging texture and consistent sameness of flavor

◆ its easy availability and wide variety of price points ($3 to $500 and more)

◆ its easy-to-pronounce name?

Its popularity with winemakers is based on:

◆ its ease of cultivation, copious yields, and hardy resistance to vine diseases

◆ its neutral character, which makes it an ideal vehicle for oak stylizing

◆ its uncanny popularity with consumers (see above)

A small number of the world's Chardonnay winemakers eschew new oak during fermentation when vinting fresh, stony Macon from Burgundy, or one or two snappy, stainless-steel fermented Chardonnays from Long Island's North Fork. At their best, these clean examples offer crisp(ish), pleasant apple and floral flavors in a medium-bodied style.

The bulk of the world's Chardonnay producers exercise no such restraint, however. Their product is rich, viscous, and heady, with aromas of fresh-baked bread, vanilla, butterscotch, and canned fruit cocktail—all the result of being outrageously revved up by fermentation and extended contact with new-oak barrels, oak chips, and powdered oak essences.

The typical Chardonnay winemaker is more chemist than vintner. Nay, more carpenter, chiefly concerned with oak: how much, how new, how charred, how long a soak? He must puzzle over weighty questions like, "What size barrels shall I use? What percentage of my wine do I ferment in them?" The wine critic, poor sap, must create unique descriptions for hundreds of the wretched concoctions, no matter that they're all virtually identical, varying only in the subtlety or ham-handedness of their oak treatment.

There are only two places that matter when considering Chardonnay, the most requested wine of our time: France and everywhere else.

The Chardonnay wines of Burgundy, such as Pouilly-Fuissé, Meursault, and the Montrachets, while offering more depth and complexity, less obvious oaking, better acidity, and earthier flavors than other Chardonnays, are, for all that, still hampered by the inherent, genetic limitations of the grape itself: modest acidity, simple flavors, and a bothersome excess of alcohol.

The primary characteristic of the rest of the world's Chardonnays is their ersatz sweetness, created by new oak. Given the choice between two wines, most consumers will consistently choose American or Australian Chardonnay over French. These sweeter wines, with their muted acidity and cloying vanilla oakiness, are exactly what they love, and producers play shamelessly to the taste. Chardonnay is the "un-white wine."

This is not to say that there are not credibly made Chardonnays from America and elsewhere, but they are few, expensive, and by and large still dominated by the taste of new oak.

Sanctuary

Thank God for Chablis! It contains the world's most northerly Chardonnay vineyards, save Champagne. The resulting higher natural acidity of its grapes and more judicious use of oak fermentation—or none at all—lifts the flinty wines of Chablis far above their peers. For me, the cool climate and chalky soils of the Chablis region engender wines that represent the epitome of Chardonnay. They drink well early and gain real depth and distinctive complexity with bottle age (say, five to seven years).

 If you must bring oaky Chardonnay to the table, build your menu around rich, sweet, nonspicy foods. Fatty fish, chicken (with its skin), and other white meats, like pork and veal, and even red meats that have had their redness cooked off (like pot roast) are all suitable food partners for this banal white wine. (Don't forget the applesauce; the acidity will help.) Believe it or not, the ultimate match for big, oaky Chardonnay is fresh, sweet corn-on-the-cob with plenty of butter.

Chablis wines, on the other hand, make superb partners for fin fish and vegetable dishes. Grown on vineyard sites composed of the detritus of ancient seabeds, the wines of Chablis also have a well-deserved reputation as fine, mineral-ly foils for snails and oysters on the half-shell.

TIPS

◆ As for ageability, it's safe to say that aside from a handful of Chardonnays from California and a few dozen from Chablis and Burgundy in "vintage of the century"–type years, Chardonnays are pretty much ready to drink within a year or two of their release and tire out frightfully fast, often in as little as three or four years after the vintage. Under-$15 Chardonnays, regardless of origin, routinely display signs of rigor by their third or fourth year.

◆ Avoid oaked Chardonnay with nonfatty fish, all shellfish, salads, and anything spicy.

◆ In general, wines made from Chardonnay, regardless of price, represent poor value, display monodimensional flavor characteristics, and offer desultory food compatibility.

SAUVIGNON BLANC

The world's most aggressive varietal—fresh, herbal, and leafy-green. Brits liken its taste to tart gooseberries and marvel at its signature "cat piss" nose. Sauvignon's nervy, acid cut and uncomplicated flavor make it a dream with seafood in general and shellfish in particular. Its mouthwatering acidity also makes it one of the world's great apéritif wines.

The touchstones for Sauvignon have always been the sister vineyards of Sancerre and Pouilly-Fumé in France's upper Loire Valley, and their cool climate and chalky soils are the reason. These wines rarely see oak, which would criminally mar the delicate purity of their fruit. Stainless-steel fermentation is the norm. While top examples actually need up to a year or so in bottle to "come together," most are best drunk up right out of the gate. Their useful lives are short—three years at best.

Farther south, in Bordeaux, the white wines of Graves are also created from Sauvignon but are rounded out with a dollop of fat, honeyed Semillon, and a lashing of new oak. With their weighty, super-earthy character, they are stylistic opposites of the lean, racy Loire Sauvignons.

Semillon is the major grape in Sauternes, the world's most acclaimed dessert wine (though only rarely its best). But the addition of 20% or 30% Sauvignon supplies the necessary acid kick to give this nectar its juicy balance and longevity.

Outside France's Loire Valley, the most happening locale for Sauvignon today has to be New Zealand. When their winemakers refrain from American-style oaking, the cut of a zesty, martini-olive-scented New Zealand Sauvignon can shame many a fine Sancerre. Take note, New Zealand winemakers: Most of the world's

Sauvignon producers would kill for your perfectly cool, maritime climate. Please don't muddy up these thrilling Sauvignons with wood just to please the timid international palate.

South Africa also holds promise as a second front for this fine, food-worthy grape. Up around $12 to $15, South African Sauvignons can achieve New Zealand–like aromatics with a fine, light elegance.

 Sauvignon's high acidity, light-to-medium body, and modest alcohol are hallmarks of a superior apéritif wine and make it an unparalleled performer with salads and vegetable dishes—even the notoriously difficult asparagus. Artichokes, which contain a chemical that turns most wines sweet and bland, can actually be tamed by a light, bone-dry Sauvignon. Its grassy, herbal personality conjures the classic marriage with chèvre (goat cheese)—herbal with herbal.

Sauvignon Blanc is a natural with seafood and makes a stellar accompaniment to shellfish. Its crisp, citrusy acids play the same part as a wedge of lemon on a seafood platter. It's also a great foil for fried and oily foods.

TIPS

◆ New Zealand and South African Sauvignons are sensational in their first year or two, but while they tend to retain their kinky, olive-like flavors, their acids can drop right out without a moment's notice. Drink 'em up.

◆ Avoid American Sauvignons, often called Fumé Blanc. The West Coast's climate is too darn hot! These Sauvignons enter the world acid-deficient and aromatically bizarre. They are immediately baptized with all manner of oak—barrels, chips, essences, and powdered extracts—that mask their aromas (probably a good idea), sweeten their flavors, and blunt what little edge is left.

◆ Sauvignon Blanc from Australia is for mutants.

CHENIN BLANC

Overlooked and underrated, Chenin Blanc produces some of the world's greatest food wines. Green and earthy, yet aromatically bright, apple-like, and tinged with vanilla, Chenin Blanc is a very grown-up taste. Chenin enjoys fantastic acidity (second only to Riesling) and surprisingly full body for a white wine with a sane alcohol level (usually around 12%). It boasts the kind of flexibility in ripening that accommodates every style, from bone-dry to off-dry to medium-sweet, all the way up through decadent dessert nectars.

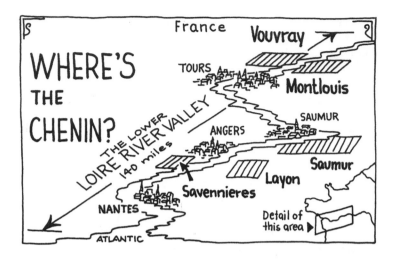

International Chenin Blanc headquarters are in the Loire Valley in northwest coastal France. Wines made here display a lovely, waxy aroma with a refreshing note of citrus and green apples.

 The most famous of all Chenin Blanc wines are born in the vineyards of Vouvray. When they are made bone-dry, *sec* will appear on the label. The classic off-dry style carries no specific label designation—simply the name Vouvray. Since every producer has his own ripeness m.o., and vintage years play a major part in sugar levels and degree of fruitiness, you'll just have to try each producer's wine. Be adventurous.

Just across the river from Vouvray lie the vineyards of Montlouis. These fascinating, little-known wines are leaner and drier than most Vouvrays and are definitely worth seeking out. Montlouis, like *sec* Vouvray, is one of the few wines of the world that have the cut to finesse briny, cold oysters on the half-shell.

On the other hand, when Chenin rots and shrivels in late autumn under the tender ministrations of the friendly fungus *botrytis cinerea,* its natural acidity helps bring critical balance to some of the most hedonistic late-harvest dessert wines on earth, like Coteaux du Layon and Bonnezeaux.

As with all wines, high acidity is an essential ingredient for aging. First-class Vouvray *sec* or *demi-sec* (dry or half-dry) can age magnificently—five or ten years is not unusual. Big, succulent wines from the vineyards of Savennières are legendary for improving for as long as fifteen or twenty years, an incredible feat for a dry white wine. Your typical, modestly priced Vouvray, though, is at its juicy best when drunk up young.

 As a versatile food partner, Chenin Blanc, along with Riesling, produces the finest, raciest, most food-flexible white wines imaginable. Their juicy acidity provides a bright, refreshing counterpoint to anything that swims, especially shellfish. Whether dinner features seafood, veal, pork, or light meat birds, Chenin Blanc's keenly balanced mouthfeel can handle it. But it's Chenin's earthy, green-leaf flavor that sets it apart from all other white varieties. When a wine can directly link up its flavor with that of vegetables and other greens, often the predominant taste in a meal, it emerges as a truly brilliant food partner. Chenin Blanc is a master of this synergy. It is also the world's best white wine grape for cream sauces.

TIPS

- If you actually lay your hands on a good $10 Vouvray, you've hit pay dirt.

- For an exhilarating culinary experience, seek out sparkling examples of Chenin Blanc for fried or oily dishes (dumplings and tapas), as well as salads and vegetables.

- Stick to France's Loire Valley for Chenin; avoid flaccid California examples and the Chenin-like thing they call Steen in South Africa.

RIESLING

The defining moment in your vinous evolution has arrived. It is time to meet Riesling. All other grape varieties are merely a prelude to the wonder of this small, fine berry. I will go into greater depth here than in any other grape chapter for two simple reasons: Riesling is the world's most important wine grape, and it creates the absolute best wines for food.

Perhaps the greatest frustration for those of us in the wine and food industry is the way that Riesling is utterly misunderstood. Is it because consumers imagine Riesling to be sickly sweet? Is it that the world's best Rieslings are grown on the steep hillsides of the Mosel and the Rhine in Germany, two locations as foreign to the American consciousness as the dark side of the moon? Is it those crazy, cryptic Teutonic labels? It's probably a bit of all of these. Never mind all that. Consider the following indisputable facts about Riesling:

1. No grape, white or red, goes better with more foods than Riesling.
2. No grape, white or red, is capable of more ethereal, complex aromatics, even at ridiculously charitable price levels of $10 to $15 a bottle.
3. No grape has higher natural acidity, across the board in all types and styles, no matter where it's grown.
4. No wine, save Moscato d'Asti, from Piedmont, or Vinho Verde, from Portugal, boasts lower alcohol levels (7% to 11% is routine).
5. No wine can be fashioned in such a fantastic array of styles and in degrees of ripeness from very dry to opulently sweet.
6. No other grape makes white wines that can age as magnificently.
7. No wine variety is more transparent in the expression of the soil in which it grows.

Riesling produces its greatest wines at the outer edge of where wine grapes can be successfully culti-vated. The riveting acid/sugar balance that is the hall-mark of great Riesling is the direct result of its struggle to ripen under difficult growing conditions, where the season is short and the sun's rays are dim. Hence, the world's best Riesling wines make their home in Germany, Alsace, and Austria.

Alsace

Alsace, which lies on the French side of the Franco-German border, produces wines very much in the French style. They are the fullest-bodied of the world's Rieslings and tend to be very dry, earthy, and high in alcohol. The most prominent name on an Alsace label is that of the grape varietal, as opposed to other French wines, which tend to highlight a vineyard or region.

Austria

The Riesling wines of eastern Austria are stylistically like Alsace, full-bodied, dry, and earthy, and only slightly less acidic. Austrian Rieslings, which are a small production wine to begin with, are grabbed up by the locals as soon as they are released, so they are somewhat difficult to find here. But they are intense, fascinating, and worth seeking out. Be prepared to pay $15 and up—when you can find them.

Germany

Germany is by far the most important source of Riesling. Her wines are the lightest, most graceful, and most fruit-expressive, as well as the most stylistically diverse.

There are five major wine-growing regions in Germany, but they all lie along or between two rivers, the Mosel and the Rhine. Riesling grapes are cultivated along the ancient chasms and sheer slopes carved out by these rivers over the millennia. Only in the few sites where the river turns to set up a hard southern exposure to the sun is the grape able to fully ripen, and then only in perhaps four years out of a decade. The key to achieving the golden ratio of sweetness and razor-sharp acidity so essential to Riesling's greatness is the grape's high natural sugar level and its cultivation in only the most desirable sites, identified by growers centuries ago. Any other grape variety planted in such hostile conditions would produce a thin, overacidic wine, even in the warmest years.

Der treacherous vineyards

THE MOSEL

Mosel Rieslings, which come in green bottles, taste of flowers, citrus, subtle autumn fruits like apples and pears, and above all, the slate on which their vineyards lie. They are the most delicate and ephemeral of all wines. (Alcohol: 7.5% to 10%)

A further definition of the wines of the Mosel would have to include the wines of the Mosel River itself and its tributaries, the Saar and the Ruwer.

- Mosel Rieslings are defined by their pronounced citrus and mineral aromatics and flavors.

- Saar Rieslings, grown in a cooler, mountainous climate, develop sensational acid cut, which affords them the longest cellaring potential. They are the steeliest of all German wines.

- Ruwer Rieslings, grown in the south of the region, are the most delicate and subtle of all Rieslings. They are sheer, filigreed, smooth as glass.

THE RHINE

Rhine Rieslings, which come in brown bottles, taste of summer fruits like apricots and peaches, berries, and currants. They are Rubenesque, tropical, and exotic. (Alcohol: 9% to 12%)

- The Nahe River is nestled between the Mosel and the Rhine. Not surprisingly, its Rieslings possess the best qualities of each: the elegance of the Mosel combined with the fleshiness of the Rhine, with a healthy dollop of stone and mineral in the mix. Nahe wines are also gorgeously aromatic, displaying exotic, nocturnal scents of honeysuckle and jasmine.

- Rheinhessen to the northwest turns out softer, plusher Rieslings with enticing aromas of wildflowers and smoky, roasted peaches. These wines represent terrific value.

◆ Rheingau Rieslings are Germany's most vigorous wines—big, drier Rieslings that make killer food partners. At their best, these historically revered wines can handle considerable cellaring and emerge with magnificent aromatics.

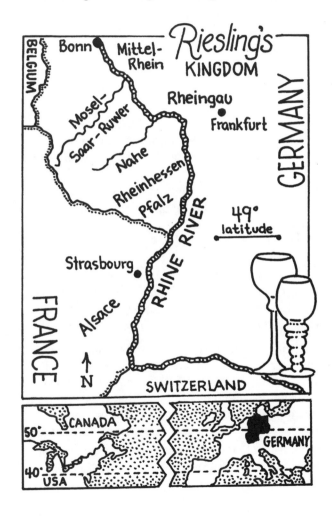

◆ The Rheinpfalz (a.k.a. the Pfalz), The Island of Dr. Moreau! The Pfalz—Germany's warmest, driest region—is also its great wine laboratory. Today it is a source of the best examples of non-Riesling Germanic varieties—i.e., Gewürztraminer, Scheurebe, Spatburgunder (Pinot Noir), and even Chardonnay. Yes, Chardonnay! Where Riesling is concerned, the Pfalz style is generous, fleshy, full, and rich, with higher alcohol (as high as 12.5%) and decidedly tropical aromas like pineapple and mango, and with a touch of grapefruit, too. Lots of excitement in the Pfalz these days.

The German Wine Label: What You Really Need to Know

The single biggest obstacle that stands between American consumers and German wines has to be language. Unlike French, Italian, and Spanish, which many Americans have studied in school or encounter occasionally in their daily lives, German is a real challenge. Even distinguishing a region or a vineyard name from that of a producer's family name can prove a daunting task. The high gothic lettering itself on traditional German wine labels shapes and distorts the words into contortions that must prove difficult even for Germans to read. That's why many wine journalists rally to the concept of simplifying German wine labels. What they forget, however, is that all that information is there for a reason. Though there are things I myself am unable to decipher on some labels, I kind of like 'em the way they are—challenging, but informative. You see, you don't need to understand every umlaut on a German wine label. You just need to be able to pick out a few words in a few key locations. The rest is all about remembering the style of producers that you really dig, and finding an enlightened wine merchant, one who knows how to buy Riesling (good luck with that).

Reading the Label: The Essentials

The single most important thing about reading a German wine label is that you're doing so in a good wineshop. If you shop in a typical neighborhood or state-run store, you can almost bet you're going to wind up with a substandard Riesling, if you can find any at all. It takes a retailer with real savvy and a first-class palate to ferret out high-quality Riesling. Like any other wine type, Riesling boasts a few very fine producers as well as plenty of dummkopfs. Only forty or fifty blue-chip producers are regularly imported, and those only by "direct import" a few times a year to serious restaurateurs and retailers. Few American wholesalers go to the trouble and expense of warehousing fine German Rieslings. Unlike Chardonnays, Cabernets and Merlots, which roll in and turn over by the freight carload, slow-selling, unloved Riesling must be special-ordered. A good wineshop will do just that, buying up the best examples at their release each autumn and spring. If you've found that special wineshop, you should now be eyeballing two or three dozen Rieslings. Let's check out some labels.

1. Grape: Look for the word *Riesling* on the German wine label. If it's not there, the wine is probably some commercial blend of lesser-quality grapes like Müller-Thurgau and Sylvaner. Liebfraumilch (made *only* for export) is definitely *not* Riesling. Rather, it is a coarse, sugary, industrial-grade fluid and should be avoided with extreme prejudice. Unfortunately, it is the very wine that consumers think of at the mention of the words *German wine*. No wonder German wine is such a tough sell.

2. Producer: In boldface type, probably at the top or at the bottom of the label, will be a family name. This is the producer, he who grew the grapes and made the wine.

3. Year: There will be a vintage date on the label, probably from the late twentieth century. Although Rieslings from good vintages can mature and develop magnificently for as much as ten or even

fifteen years, most are meant to be drunk up in their first five or six. It is this ageability factor that can add real thrills to the occasional discovery of a forgotten bottle of older Riesling. Only the track record of a given producer and the attributes of a specific vintage can indicate a Riesling's potential longevity. Consult your wine merchant.

4. Place: The next size typeface will be the town (with an *"er"* after it—such as *Niersteiner*—from the town of Nierstein). And then the vineyard within the town (such as Niersteiner Orbel—from the Orbel vineyard). These specific vineyards, capable of conferring distinct stylistic attributes to the wines vinified from them, are as important for you to know as the name of the producer. A great producer can sometimes create fantastic wine at less than highly rated vineyard sites and in less than great years. On the other hand, most first-class German producers whose wines are imported here do happen to make their wines in many of the best vineyards (defined by microclimate, drainage, angle to the sun, etc.).

5. Alcohol: Alcohol in wine is generated by enzymes created by grape skin yeasts reacting with grape juice sugars during fermentation. If a wine is allowed to ferment "out" fully, all of its sugars will be converted to alcohol; hence, a dry, fuller-bodied wine of high alcohol (11% or more for Riesling). If the fermentation process is shortened (halted by lowering the temperature of the fermenting juice), less of the grape sugars will be consumed; hence, a sweeter, lighter-bodied wine of lower alcohol (10% or less for Riesling). So, in the case of German Riesling, regardless of other label information, a wine's alcohol level speaks volumes about how sweet-and-light or dry-and-rich it will be.

6. Ripeness: Unless you plan to devote considerable effort to the study of German vineyards and producers, what you really need to know is the *style* of the wine you'd like to serve with a given meal. Somewhere on the label in fairly large letters will be a ripeness designation. This denotes the level of ripeness at which the grapes

were picked, and consequently the sweetness, body, and acidity of the final product.

Kabinett (dry to off-dry): racy, light-to-medium body, little or no sweetness. Elegant.

Spätlese (riper, off-dry): fuller body, fruitier, juicier. Thrilling when well made.

Auslese (very ripe): light-to-medium body, yet not too sweet for rich entrées. The aging process diminishes an Aulese Riesling's youthful sweetness, resulting in a succulent, yet vibrant white wine that dwarfs all others as a choice for rich fish and white meat preparations. Mature Auslese Rieslings make superior choices in these instances to most light red wines.

Beerenauslese (B.A.) (luscious and sweet): from selected late-harvested, shriveled bunches of grapes. Ethereal dessert wines.

Trockenbeerenauslese (T.B.A.) (unctuous, very sweet and concentrated): from selected late-harvested, shriveled *individual* grapes. Sweet, vinous Valhalla.

Eiswein (Ice Wine) (ultrasweet with uncanny acidity): from late-harvested grapes picked frozen. What little water remains is hung up in the press as ice. The remaining juice is pure fruit extract, sweetness, and acidity. A high-wire balancing act of power and finesse.

A dry idea: Two subcategories that may appear on Kabinett and Spätlese labels are:

Trocken (literally "dry"): nearly zero residual sugar, drier and crisper than the driest Sauvignon Blanc.

Halbtrocken (literally "half-dry"): significant body and richness, yet still essentially dry.

In a sort of perverse reversal of what happened in the early 1980s, when California vintners literally left thousands of acres of Zinfandel grapes hanging on the vine because of the lack of consumer interest, German wine producers, perhaps out of a similar sense of desperation, came up with what they thought might be an effective way of changing the public's mind about Riesling. In California, they began to bottle their unwanted red Zinfandel as a sweet, pink, pop wine and wound up with a marketing sensation: White Zinfandel. The Germans, on the other hand, figuring that "drying up" their great, fruity Rieslings would find them a wider market, began to encourage lengthier fermentations (fermenting out sugars and creating bigger, drier Rieslings). The unexpected yet happy result was a unique addition to the culinary landscape: yet another style of Riesling. This overcame Riesling's only remaining weak spot at the table, that of a counterweight to rich sauces, raw or fatty fish, and briny shellfish, a feat now smartly handled by Trocken (dry) and Halbtrocken (half-dry) Rieslings.

Nothing, I repeat, *nothing* marries better with more foods than Riesling. Alsatian and Austrian examples make fine partners for all richly sauced fatty fish, white meats, and sausages, but because of their out-sized body and alcohol, they should be reserved for only the richest fare. When it comes to overall wine and food compatibility, there is absolutely nothing that any single white wine variety can do for food that a German Riesling can't do better. Whereas other white wine varieties might be generally serviceable with food, German Rieslings fairly sing at the table. I have found that when enlightened drinkers discover the complexity and finesse of German Rieslings with food, they begin to lose interest in other varieties, sort of the way musical taste evolves in the maturing adult—say, from KISS to Korngold. Frankly, I find that even a mediocre German Riesling beats all hell out of most other grape varieties at the table. In other words, nearly any Riesling is better than none.

While Kabinett-level Rieslings will support and complement virtually all seafood and vegetable dishes, as well as a host of Asian foods, riper Spätlese Rieslings, when served with chicken and white meats (pork and veal), are often superior choices, even superior to light reds, because of their better acidity and subtler flavors. Needless to say, Riesling's bright acidity, delicate sweetness, and low alcohol make it the mother of all spicy food partners. Try luscious Auslese Rieslings alongside Asian dishes that contain coconut milk or a honey mustard base, as well as with sweet appetizers, from glazed chicken wings to sautéed foie gras. It eroticizes your grandmother's holiday ham (if you're into that sort of thing). And if you close your eyes and pour yourself a glass of rich Spätlese- or Auslese-grade Riesling alongside a hunk of red meat, what's truly astounding is how perversely delicious they taste together. But keep your eyes closed. The concept of white wine with red meat might short-circuit your neural transmitters.

Anyway, try a German Riesling at dinner alongside a comparably priced Chardonnay—French, Californian, or Australian. The Chardonnay will seem dull and leaden, while the Riesling will be light and mouthwatering. The Chardonnay wine, with its ponderous oak treatment and excessive alcohol, will obscure subtle food flavors, while the Riesling will amplify them. You be the judge.

If Riesling is the world's greatest food wine—and be certain, it is—then Riesling Sekt (sparkling) must be the greatest of all food partners that bubble. I rank sparkling Loire Chenin, Crémant d'Alsace (Pinot Blanc), and Prosecco from Italy's Veneto as superb apéritif wines. They are also wonderful, light, high-acid accompaniments to a world of deep-fried, sautéed, and other oily preparations, as well as great foils for egg dishes, soups, and salads. But first-class Riesling Sekt will straddle more of these food challenges than any one of these sparkling wines. No one adores great Champagne more than I, but with its fuller body from Chardonnnay and Pinot Noir, and more penetrating mousse, Champagne is a sparkling wine of somewhat limited food uses.

TIPS

◆ There has never been a better time to discover and to revel in the joys of German Riesling. Germany has enjoyed a string of very good to superb vintages spanning nine years, an occasion literally unparalleled in the entire recorded history of the region (thanks to unusually great weather, better winemaking, and, I don't know—el Niño?).

◆ Considering the breadth of the American continent and its many successful wine-growing regions, most of what lies west of New York State is a Riesling wasteland, including the irrigated desert that is Washington State, whose efforts tend to result in wines that are vaguely Rieslinglike but remain spineless and cloyingly sweet. The Finger Lakes region of New York State is where Riesling really kicks butt in the U.S. of A. At $10 to $12 a bottle, they show lots of class and drink beautifully with nearly everything.

◆ By and large, you'll have an easier time finding complimentary foie gras than Riesling in most restaurants. If your favorite restaurant has no Riesling on its list, suggest one for them. If they do offer one or two, badger them for more. Failing that, bring your own!

◆ America's few major importers of first-class German wine estates have recently begun to align themselves with conscientious distributors who get their wines into better wineshops. Shop around. Seize the moment.

◆ *Weingut* on a German wine label doesn't mean "wine that's good," and it's not like a beer belly. It means *winery* and will generally precede the name of the producer on the label.

I sometimes find myself torn between the desire to share the sublime joys of Riesling with the entire known world or greedily keep mum so that Riesling's ridiculously low price and great availability will remain as they are today. A smart shopper can purchase seriously outrageous Riesling, wines of real style, for a mere $10 to $15 a bottle. At $20, they blow the doors off all other white wines. Wait a minute—why the hell am I telling *you* this?

UND . . . OTHER GERMANIC GRAPES

Gewürztraminer

The grape that people love trying to pronounce (it's geh-VERTZ-trah-meen-er, or else geh-vertz-TRAH-mun-er if you're British). *Würz* means "spicy," which describes its most prescient characteristic. Gewürztraminers are full-bodied, oily-textured wines that boast an outrageous scent, dominated by rose petals and that honey-sweet, exotic Asian nutmeat known as lychee (pronounced LIE-chee). Most Gewürztraminer is made in a dry to off-dry style, though honeyed dessert-wine versions can be breathtaking.

 Like Riesling, Gewürztraminer excels in the cool climes of Alsace and Germany but is generally known as that big, spicy Alsatian grape. When Alsace Gewürztraminer is on target, it boasts a rosy bouquet, viscous mouthfeel, and a seemingly endless length of flavor. High alcohol levels, though, can be a problem (13 to 14% are common). In such cases, these wines practically require a knife and fork.

In my exploration of German wines, a happy bonus has been the discovery of German Gewürztraminer from the Pfalz region, only occasionally encountered here. Actually, Pfalz is said to have supplied the very source cuttings for much of today's Alsace Gewürztraminer. German Gewürztraminers, however, are lighter and fruitier, and possess the ever-desirable combo of good acid, modest sweetness, and low alcohol (9 to 10%). Also, while Alsace Gewürztraminer enters the market at around $13 to $15, Pfalz Gewürztraminer begins at $10.

 The full body, high alcohol, and pungent, spicy fruit of Alsace Gewürztraminer marries well with bold, herb-seasoned sausages, alliaceous dishes (heavy on the onions, garlic, chives, or shallots), and roasted poultry and white meats (veal and pork), in rich sauces. In Alsace, Gewürz is terrific with the ubiquitous *choucroute garni* (sausages and other meats on a bed of steaming sauerkraut). It's also a nice match with smoked fish and cheeses.

German Gewürztraminer is far more food-flexible. It handles the above fairly well, but its lighter body and low alcohol allow it to straddle Asian cuisines like Chinese, Thai, and even Indian. A 9% alcohol Gewürztraminer, especially a ripe Spätlese- or Auslese-level wine, has few peers with spicy versions of the above foods.

TIPS

◆ Don't panic if the Gewürz in your glass has deeper color than other white wines. This is merely the result of contact with its dark pink skins.

◆ Contrary to the prevailing myth, Alsace Gewürztraminer should be the last wine of choice for Chinese food—the spicy kind, anyway. Too much alcohol for this grub.

◆ Some feel there is great potential for the grape in America's Pacific Northwest. Many also believe that the tooth fairy still owes them $5.

Scheurebe

Scheurebe (SHOY-ray-beh)—a bright, juicy, wonderfully fragrant grape—is a cross between Riesling and Silvaner, created by a Dr. Georg Scheu (rebe simply means grape). In well-made versions, its aromas are redolent of black currants and citrus, and its mouthfeel is nearly as exciting and refreshing as that of Riesling. Alcohol is nominal, at around 10%. Ripeness designations are the same as those used with Riesling, running in sweetness from Kabinett (driest) up through Spätlese (riper), Auslese (very ripe), and on up into dessert-grade levels.

Scheurebe is found mainly in Germany's Rhein-hessen and Pfalz. Not much Scheurebe is being grown now (about 10,000 acres), but one or two conscientious importers are now offering it in the American market.

Kabinetts and Spätleses go with a variety of richly flavored foods but especially with spicy fare. Dessert-grade Scheurebe is a pungent and exotic accompaniment to any sort of tart, custard, or candied fruit.

TIPS

◆ Prices range from $10 Kabinetts up through fascinating $25 to $35 examples. If you spot one at any price, grab it.

◆ Dessert wines (Beerenauslese and Trockenbeerenauslese) made from Scheurebe are terrific value, as they tend to be less expensive than their Riesling cousins.

Gruner Veltliner

Gruner Veltliner, or "Gruner!," as we say, is a fine, adult beverage. While drinking Gruner will not keep the landlord from your door or encourage small dogs and smiling children to follow you about, this firm, fragrant, penetrating dry white wine from Austria can't help but enrich your gustatory life. There's something faintly earthy and delicate in Gruner's aroma, something floral and sometimes herbaceous. There's also a white pepper thing and just a hint of peach. Although its aroma is complex and difficult to describe, Gruner's lovely balance and elegant mouthfeel are irresistible.

Austria is *it* for Gruner Veltliner. It is the predominant grape there and makes wine at quality levels that begin with fresh, delightful $10 one-liter bottlings and climb to impeccably elegant wines at a mere $15 or $20. The Gruners that are available today in the U.S. are primarily from small, artisanal winemaking families and represent the highest quality level. Get some! *Now!*

Serve Gruner with herbed fish, of course, and delicate white meats and poultry. Sautéed greens are a terrific match, and mollusks such as oysters, scallops, and snails. Try one with a simple pasta of garlic, oil, and sautéed wild mushrooms. With its modest alcohol, crisp fruit, and light-as-a-feather personality, Gruner stands with Riesling and Chenin Blanc as one of the world's most delightful and versatile white wines.

TIPS

- ◆ Gruner Veltliner can be enjoyed young, or aged nearly as long as fine Riesling—even ten or fifteen years.
- ◆ Don't be disappointed if you can't find Gruner. You may need to visit one of those ritzy midtown wineshops that cater to well-heeled muckety-mucks from vague Middle European duchies. Persevere.

Reds

MERLOT

It's what people are clamoring for, what they crave. Grape growers can't grow enough, sales reps can't sell enough, restaurateurs can't mark it up enough. It's new, it's hip, it's now, it's wow! It's hi-fi, it's sci-fi, it's E. coli!

When I sat down to describe Merlot, I realized the most succinct definition had already been written. What follows is the complete, unabridged entry for Merlot in the latest edition of Alexis Lichine's exhaustive, eight-hundred-page *New Encyclopedia of Wines & Spirits* (Alfred Knopf, 1987). This is the same "bible" we wine salespeople cut our teeth on in the 1970s.

> Merlot: The blue-black, thick-skinned grape which imparts softness and roundness to the red wines of the Medoc district in Bordeaux. This grape is grown also in Italy, Switzerland, Chile, a little in California, and elsewhere.

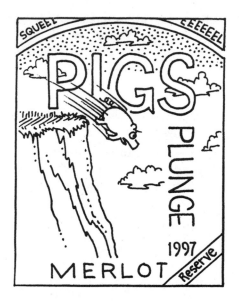

That's it. I guess he gave it the attention he felt it merited.

So what the hell happened to make this innocuous, also-ran variety the rampaging wildebeest of the wine world?

- ◆ As a red grape, Merlot is the "un-red wine," the twin to Chardonnay in its use as a neutral, low-acid base for oak flavoring.

- ◆ Like Chardonnay, Merlot has a one-dimensional flavor profile (some nonspecific mélange of plumlike fruits liberally dosed with chocolaty oak).

- ◆ Like Chardonnay, they all taste virtually the same—like wood.

- ◆ Prices range from $3.99 for Chilean examples to $600 for Bordeaux's vaunted Château Petrus. Ye gods! Alexis Lichine must be spinning in his grave.

It's everywhere—from Bordeaux to Bulgaria, from California to Kazhakstan, wherever money is to be made from wine. They're tearing up old-vine Zinfandel and Petite Sirah by the acre in California, and Syrah and Grenache by the hectare in southern France, and inserting Merlot as if it were some great miracle crop that will finally feed the world's poor.

The two main sources for premium Merlot wines are Bordeaux in France and the West Coast of the United States. In Bordeaux, most of the château wines are primarily based on Cabernet Sauvignon with some amount of Merlot blended in for softening. On the east bank of the Gironde, the smaller part of Bordeaux, lie St.-Emilion and Pomerol, whose wines are Merlot-based, with some Cabernet Sauvignon and Cabernet Franc for strength and flavor. Even mediocre wines from St.-Emilion and Pomerol command absurdly high prices ($25 to $50).

Viticulture's Finest Hour

Merlonnay

The best Merlots from America are those punched up liberally with Cabernet Sauvignon and/or Cabernet Franc, although the oaking of these wines is generally so thorough that it hardly makes a difference. Expect to pay over $25 for high-scoring wines.

♦ Get a life.

CABERNET SAUVIGNON

Numero Uno, King of the Hill, El Capitaine, the Big Taco. Call me . . . Cab. (Or call me a cab.) Cabernet is the preferred grape for wines destined for the cellar. By itself or blended with Merlot and Cabernet Franc, it creates wines that are occasionally capable of improving with age for as long as a century. Most, though ($10 and under), are happily ready to drink in two or three years and gain little from additional time in bottle.

Cabernet Sauvignon, a grape whose DNA parentage has recently been revealed as Sauvignon Blanc and Cabernet Franc— *sacre bleu!*—is a small, thick-skinned black berry. Wines made from it taste of black fruits (black cherries, currants, and black raspberries), mint, earth, and vanilla (from new oak). Its thick skins and traditional wood aging are its dual sources of tannins, which are the key to its longevity. The dry, puckery mouthfeel produced by young Cabernet Sauvignon is a function of these tannins. Over time, they fall out of the solution as sediment, leaving a soft, velvety wine behind. The secondary aromas and flavors that emerge with maturity are earth (fungi and forest floor), spice (cinnamon, pepper), and tobacco (cigar box).

Cabernet Sauvignon is the exemplar of the red wine grape that faithfully expresses its soil of origin (*terroir*). When grown responsibly (yields kept to a minimum, judicious oaking, etc.), the wines of specific regions in Bordeaux, California, and Australia—like Pauillac, Rutherford, and Coonawara—each reflect their individual appellations. Other Cabernet wines of the world, by and large, lack

this clear geographic touchstone. They taste as if they could have been grown anywhere.

Cabernet falls into two distinct flavor profiles:

1. The Bordeaux Style: blended with Merlot and Cabernet Franc in varying degrees; oaky and tannic when young; restrained, subtle fruit emerges with proper cellaring; deep, earthy, and complex. These are the Châteaux wines of Bordeaux, France.

2. The International Style. Although modeled everywhere after the wines of Bordeaux, emerging international pop tastes in the early 1970s dictated an inevitable swing toward a sweeter, more accessible flavor profile. The result: mostly monovarietal wines (100% Cabernet); oaky and tannic when young, like Bordeaux, but with sweeter, more up-front, jammy fruit unless aged—which 98% of this style Cabernet isn't. With their in-your-face fruit and creamy oak sweetness, these wines are all about immediate gratification (hence, the lack of auction or investment activity, save for a dozen or so high-profile California properties). Included are wines from California, Australia, New Zealand, South America, Italy, South Africa, Eastern Europe, and elsewhere.

Bordeaux-style Cabernet blends are deep, curranty wines with plenty of body, aroma, and length of flavor. They are the classical partners for French haute cuisine, including rich sauces and dishes focused on beef, lamb, duck, and other game birds. Mature versions can be served with lighter meats (pork and veal) and white-meat birds when richly sauced.

The international-style Cabernets, best represented by California, may also be served with richly sauced fare and most red meats and game birds. Though serviceable companions to subtle, complex food preparations, they really rock with burgers and ribs.

In short, Cabernet Sauvignon can't be beat alongside hearty, unctuous cuisines, like steaks, chops, and Sunday roasts, but woe to those who stray beyond these culinary borders. Cabernet is a big, hefty brute that takes over at the table, running roughshod over most everyday foods, obliterating all flavor and nuance.

TIPS

◆ As with all full-bodied, high-alcohol, oaky wines, avoid Cabernet Sauvignon with spicy foods, cream and tomato sauces, delicate vegetables, and anything that swims.

◆ In Bordeaux, no matter what they say about technological advances in the vineyard and winery, no matter what they say about "no more bad vintages," even in summers with too little sun and too much rain, when the weather stinks in Bordeaux, its wines are weedy and thin, representing horrific value.

SANGIOVESE

Sangiovese ("blood of Jove") is not so much one grape as a family of grapes that share a common genetic origin. Winemakers refer to the various clones of Sangiovese by their regional synonyms. In Chianti, it's known simply as Sangiovese. But Prugnolo Gentile is Sangiovese in Montepulciano; the Brunello clone is Sangiovese in Montalcino; in Emilio-Romagna, it's Sangiovese Romagna; while in southern Tuscany the local name is Morellino.

Given the variety of clones, vintage sensitivity, and quality extremes, Sangiovese remains a diverse and elusive variety. While the greatest examples evoke beguiling aromas of berry fruits and spice, they still possess a coarse earthiness that hints at the ancient (possibly Etruscan) origin of Sangiovese.

Although Sangiovese is the most widely planted red variety in Italy, it is in Tuscany that its fame is founded. It represents an integral ingredient in no fewer than twenty of Tuscany's wine-growing appellations, the most renowned of which are Brunello di Montalcino and Chianti.

Lighter examples of Sangiovese, including inexpensive Chiantis, are fine partners for *fagiole* (Tuscan bean dishes), pasta with simple red sauces, pizza, and the salty, cured meats of central Italy (e.g., prosciutto and pancetta).

Save the opulent Brunello di Montalcino and Vino Nobile di Montepulciano for such intensely flavored foods as game birds, grilled meats (aged steaks, especially), and *grana* (hard) cheeses, such as Parmesan and asiago, as well as the great Tuscan pecorino.

TIPS

◆ Because of its naturally high acidity and tannin, Sangiovese is super sensitive to the vintage. It ripens poorly in any but the hottest, driest years, resulting in one nasty, astringent brute of a red wine—hence, the common complaint about many typically unripe Chiantis.

◆ Unfortunately, most Chianti lives up to its bad reputation. A sure test of your wine merchant's dedication and tasting savvy is his ability to ferret out good Chianti—at any price point.

◆ Although excellent with tomato sauce–based preparations, because of its fine acidity and sweetness, Sangiovese is a relatively subtle variety and so can never offer the more dynamic cut and fruit impact of good Barbera.

◆ As an alternative to Brunello, routinely $40 to $50 a bottle and rarely worth it, try Rosso di Montalcino, sometimes called Baby Brunello ($10 to $20) or the traditional Sangiovese-Cabernet blend from Tuscany, Carmignano ($15 to $30).

◆ Super Tuscans: Enriched with Cabernet Sauvignon, hammered with sweet new oak, and gussied up in designer bottles with punts deep enough to spend the night in, so-called Super Tuscans are all too often Italy's entry in a field of wildly overpriced, award-winning red wine gorillas.

NEBBIOLO

Barolo, the fabled king of Italian red wines, is the ultimate expression of the Nebbiolo grape. To taste a twenty-year-old Barolo from a good producer in a great vintage is to be thunderstruck by a mélange of aromas that exist nowhere else in Italian wine. Swirling up from the glass come scents of moist earth, tar, herbs, and truffles, wrapped in a potpourri of faded violets and garden roses. In the mouth it is lush, massive, and utterly satisfying.

Yes, I recall actually having such a wine once . . . just once. Today, Barolos like the one above are being held hostage in the cellars of nuclear lawyers and orthodontists. When monumental Barolos are vinted (sadly, only once or twice in a decade), they are gobbled up by well-heeled collectors before they ever see the inside of a wineshop. Barolos from other years are generally hard, ungenerous, and green. These "off-vintage" dogs are hardly worth $10 a bottle, no less their brazen $30 or $40 selling prices.

A "new school" of Barolo winemakers is using shorter fermentations and small French oak barrels for aging rather than the traditional long fermentation and three- or four-year sojourn in enormous Slovenian casks. In this way, the modernists emphasize a softer, fruitier style of wine that can be drunk sooner; however, their wines from off vintages are just as crummy as old-style Barolos—only oakier.

Italy's second "great" Nebbiolo wine is Barolo's neighboring vineyard, Barbaresco, theoretically fruitier and more supple than

Barolo, though equally overpriced and fraught with expensive duds. Wines labeled *Spanna* (a local synonym for Nebbiolo) can offer real richness and value at $10 to $15 but also only in those choice years. Gattinara, which is fun to pronounce and has a certain cachet due to its stylized bladder-like bottle, is one of the last bastions of old-style, "dirty barrel" winemaking—and usually tastes it.

With its hot summers and dense autumn fogs—the *nebbia* (nebula, nebulous, et al.) from which Nebbiolo takes its name—Piedmont, in northwest Italy, is the natural home for this fascinating but frustrating variety.

Serve with game, roasted red meats, especially lamb, and dishes with strong mushroom flavors. With its erotic, earthy perfume, the Albanese white truffle is Barolo's greatest match. A simple chunk of pecorino is not a bad idea, either.

TIPS

- Traditionally made Barolos and Barbarescos from fine vintages require at least a decade to shed their tannic cloak and begin to reveal their special aromatic charms.
- In less-than-great years, Baroli and Barbaresci are a waste of moni.

SYRAH

Syrah is the third "noble" red wine grape of France, along with Cabernet Sauvignon and Pinot Noir. It is a dark, thick-skinned grape that requires hot, dry ripening conditions to balance its weight with sweetness. The large-scaled wines made from Syrah benefit from the mild oxidation that occurs during oak aging, and once in bottle are capable of a long, graceful maturation.

A glass of Syrah can be like breakfast at the IHOP: Billowing out of the glass come aromas of blueberry pancakes, maple syrup, and smoky bacon. Also, the thick, telltale scent of lilies and fresh herbs.

 The agreed archetype for 100 percent Syrah wine is the tiny northern Rhône Valley in southeastern France. Its two legendary vineyard areas are the stony, steep, terraced hills known as Hermitage and Côte Rôtie. Hermitage is a big, beefy sumo wrestler of a wine—when young, that is. With ten years in a cool cellar, it emerges a refined gentleman: deep, earthy, and elegant. Côte Rôtie ("roasted slope") offers a sappy fragrance of raspberries, game, and bacon sizzling in the pan. Côte Rôtie also requires a decade or so in bottle to fulfill its promise.

Australia and California are also creating very good Syrah wines today but in a far different style. Given new winemaking techniques and the need for warm growing locations for Syrah, these regions represent near-perfect environments. Australian and Californian versions have their own positive attributes—among them, earlier drinkability and greater food versatility, due to their sweeter flavors and softer tannins.

In Australia, Syrah, known as Shiraz, has been cultivated since 1837, primarily as a source for sweet, late-harvest, port-style wines. Only since the 1960s has a serious effort been made to produce dry table wines. The result is that Shiraz (Syrah) has now become Australia's defining contribution to the world of red wines. Its sweet pot-of-jam flavor and plush, velvety mouthfeel make it irresistible to nearly everyone.

If ever there was an example of a country grooming an industry for success, it is Australia. By setting high tariffs on imported wines, thereby limiting their number and selection, and so inflating their prices, they have created a flourishing home-grown wine industry that is the envy of other wine-producing nations. Australians adore their sweet, ripe native wines largely, I believe, because they can't find any others.

Over the past ten years or so, first-class Australian Shiraz at around $10 a bottle has represented some of the best red wine value in the American market. Well, the party's over. Today, that $10 bottle is almost $20, and deluxe models will set you back more like $40. It has now become nearly impossible to find affordable high-quality Shiraz. Even that $20 Shiraz now features less fruit extraction and more oak flavoring to camouflage its absence. Overtaxing their vines to meet growing world demand, major Australian wine corporations are finally distilling higher profits from greed and oak chips.

As for California, all the unwarranted, slavish adoration given to Merlot should be refocused on Syrah. The grape seems to thrive there, and since it handles wood so smartly, it's a natural in the hands of West Coast oak-meisters. Stylistically, these Syrah wines fall somewhere between the roasty Rhônes and the jammy Aussies: deep, yet fruity and fairly elegant. They begin around $10 and top out at about $30. This makes them better wines than Merlot and better values than Cabernet.

Light, fruity California Syrah and Australian Shiraz are just fine with ketchupy burgers, roast chicken, pizza, and other everyday fare, sans seafood. Plumper wines from these locations stand up beautifully to barbecue and Peking duck. Dark, brooding Rhône examples need dark, brooding foods, like venison, boar, and game birds (duck, goose, or well-hung woodcock). Sorry.

TIPS

◆ Look for Cornas, the tiny, oft-forgotten alternative to Côte Rôtie and Hermitage. Good Cornas, for me, represents the purest, unstylized Syrah wine. Crozes-Hermitage, the area adjacent to the vineyard of Hermitage itself, can be a fine value at about $15 a bottle.

♦ Syrah is also blended with the wildly popular Grenache, which forms the base of countless hot climate reds, chief among them Châteauneuf du Pape.

Throughout southwestern France, lesser grapes are being uprooted in favor of Syrah, where its addition to the blend in appellations like Corbières, Minervois, and Saint-Chinian is creating a new wave of world-class red wine bargains—and not a minute too soon.

ZINFANDEL

America's wine! Big, black, beautiful Zinfandel embodies the American experience. An immigrant with not one but two funny-sounding names (Plavac Mali from Croatia, or Primitivo from Apulia), Zinfandel (which coincidentally rhymes with "sin" and "fun" and "hell") arrived in California over a century ago, where nostalgic Italian farmers with names like Sebastiani, Pedroncelli, and Martini used it to recreate the heady, full-bodied reds of their homeland. Ours is the blessed generation that gets to drink Zinfandel that's grown on those very same ancient, gnarled vines. Wines made from such hoary old vines can be rare and cost as much as $30 or $40 a bottle.

Zinfandel's jammy, in-your-face flavor, oft described as "brambly" (bramble fruits like raspberries and blackberries), makes it America's most decadent red. At its best, it is obscenely rich and succulent, with soft tannins and good acidity. More often, it's as big as a house, oaked to oblivion, and alcoholic enough to singe your nostril hairs.

 Zinfandel grows throughout California but excels in the warm, high-elevation vineyards of Sonoma, Amador, and Paso Robles. In Apulia (the "heel" of the

Italian boot) it's known as Primitivo and behaves appropriately, like some hairy half-simian, reeking of sweat and roadkill. Try one sometime.

Do not drink Zinfandel with cream sauces, light fish or shellfish, white meats (unless well grilled or blackened), or spicy foods. Its body and alcohol are much too high. *Do* drink it with nonspicy barbecue, burgers, takeout chickens, red meats, and game birds. Zinfandel is my personal favorite with grilled dogs, ribs, and burgers on the Fourth. In its late-harvest incarnation, it stops the show after dinner with chocolate or hard, salty cheeses. In its Italian late-harvest version, the rare, truly sinful Primitivo Dolce di Manduria, its sultry sweetness and velvety mouthfeel rival those of fine vintage port.

TIPS

◆ Expect to pay over $10 for good entry-level Zinfandel. Serious quality begins at around $16 and peaks with the best examples at $25 to $35. These few, plush, premium Zinfandels come into the market rarely (only once or twice a year). They are highly allocated. You'll need to call around for them and move quickly when they turn up. A major part of Zinfandel's charm is its youthful exuberance. While weightier "big name" Zins may appear to show potential for longevity, rarely do they improve much past four or five years.

PINOT NOIR

Pinot ("noir" is for amateurs) would surely produce the world's most versatile food wine—were it not for a grape named Riesling. But Pinot can deal with red meat—a feat even Riesling can't number among its bag of tricks. And it can make the sexiest red wines on earth . . . sometimes.

As a crop, Pinot can be a winemaker's ball and chain. It ripens too early, it requires an extra-long growing season in a coolish climate, and yields must be kept punishingly low in order to extract its elusive magic. Pinot is abnormally susceptible to gray rot, powdery mildew, and a nasty agri-bummer called leaf roll. (If you've ever had that, you know how embarrassing it can be.)

 The grape seems to excel in two places: in the vineyards of Burgundy in northeastern France and in cooler areas of the West Coast of the United States. These two locations produce two very different styles.

Burgundy (Bourgogne)

If opera is entertainment for grown-ups, then Burgundy must be the red wine equivalent of Giuseppe Verdi. Mature, passionate wine lovers invariably choose it over all others—probably for these reasons:

1. Its complexity, beguiling sweetness, and exquisite texture and length
2. Its sublime compatibility with upscale cuisine
3. Its prohibitively high price, which discourages the peasants

The price level is due more to scarcity than quality. Burgundy is a relatively small vineyard area, and its percentage of really fine wines is painfully small. When collectors in New York, London, and Tokyo are willing to shell out thousands at auction for even a dreadful vintage, quality becomes a side issue. Furthermore, many Burgundians prey on public ignorance. Any yahoo with twenty vines in Gevrey Chambertin can flagrantly overproduce (more juice per vine plant equals less quality) and take advantage of a famous place name to price his bottles on a par with more serious producers. Without the benefit of a well-informed wine adviser, a typical consumer has little chance of finding the gems of the region. It is for these reasons that top Burgundy might be called the world's riskiest wine purchase.

Burgundy is divided into two halves. In the north lies the Côtes du Nuits, home of big, sappy, inky wines structured for hefty foods and long aging. In the south, the Côte de Beaune produces graceful, elegant, more delicately styled wines.

American

Quality American Pinot is a rather recent phenomenon, as vine plantings, as well as winemaking skills, have finally begun to mature. The best-chosen microclimates for the cultivation of Pinot are in California's Central Coast, Carneros and Russian River, and Oregon, where cool evenings, misty mornings, and warm, sunny afternoons favor this fickle grape. American Pinots tend to be sweeter than their French counterparts, which helps them perform admirably at the table. Unfortunately, many examples are still plagued by a lack of richness and an excess of alcohol and oak, which can make them quite nasty, with or without food.

 At its best, Pinot epitomizes the twin pillars of wine-food compatibility: acidity and sweetness. Typical California examples and lighter-style Burgundies tend to offer the juicy acids and lowish tannin and alcohol levels that work beautifully with light meats, tomato-based sauces, and fish of every stripe. More formidable Burgundies and weightier Oregon Pinots are classic accompaniments for duck, goose, and wild game, especially where some sweetness has been introduced, through grill marks or glazes.

TIPS

◆ Other regions: Overpriced examples of Pinot from northern Italy or Australia are rarely worth drinking—at any price. Actually, Pinot may be the only grape variety on earth that flourishes in almost as few places as Riesling.

- Look for the classic *goût de terroir* ("taste of the earth"), or more apt, "barnyard on a warm summer day" aroma of great Burgundy and occasional American Pinots.
- Be wary of American Pinots with more than 13% alcohol.
- Most Burgundy begins to drink well after five or six years in bottle; American wines in three or four.
- Wine insiders simply call it Pinot, and so will you if you want respect.

BARBERA

Ah, Barbera! A grape I can relate to. Its hallmarks are mouth-cleansing acidity, modest alcohol, soft tannins, and vibrant red-cherry sweetness, all elements that give it a place of honor at the table. It produces a dark red wine in a wide variety of styles, from fresh and fruity ($8 to $12) to deep and profound ($15 to $20 and up). It also fleshes out nicely with oak aging, sometimes producing stunning, complex examples (referred to in the trade as "barrique-aged Barberas").

 Barbera is the second most widely planted red wine variety in Italy behind Sangiovese (the grape of Chianti and Brunello) and the most planted grape in Piedmont, in northern Italy. This is Barbera's native home, where it thrives alongside the region's more ballyhooed celebrity, the difficult, cerebral Nebbiolo (the grape of Barolo, Barbaresco, and Gattinara).

Ten thousand acres are planted in California, mostly in its warmer areas (San Joaquin Valley, etc.), where it adds zest to oceans of inexpensive jug wines.

 For those who appreciate mouthwatering acidity in white wines (and who doesn't?), Barbera is *your* red. It revels in the most difficult culinary challenges, especially in the wine-bending arena of tomato sauce. Only citrus fruits contain higher acidity than tomatoes, and only Barbera offers high enough acidity to sluice through red sauce with its personality still intact. Its sweet red-berry flavor can shine through even the most highly seasoned and spicy preparations. No Italian red can take on cream sauces as handily as Barbera. Try one with a grilled whole fish, any kind of sausages, or Chinese food—hot or not.

TIPS

- Fresh, juicy, inexpensive versions are eminently chillable.
- Like other high-acid wines, poor examples can be particularly heinous. Watch out!

GAMAY

Gamay *is* Beaujolais, and Beaujolais is that elusive, sought-after prize: a red wine food partner that behaves like a white. It's cherished for its fresh, uncomplicated fruit and bright red-cherry aroma. The most versatile red wine in France, and perhaps the world, it is the definitive light red: high in fruit and natural acidity, low in alcohol, utterly fresh and quaffable.

Over 70 percent of all Beaujolais exported is called *Nouveau Beaujolais,* made by a method called carbonic maceration, which means the grapes were fermented without oxygen, uncrushed, and in whole bunches. Fermentation takes place quickly, in just four days. Grapes are heaped atop one another in giant closed, steel-fermenting vessels until the bottom 20 or 30 percent are crushed beneath their own weight. As the spilled juice begins fermenting, carbon dioxide (a by-product) rises up in the tank, where it causes the balance of the grapes, still whole, to begin fermenting while still in their skins. The result is a wine of explosive ripe fruit, low alcohol, and light body, with a soft, juicy mouthfeel. Pure fun.

The Beaujolais appellation produces more than 60 percent of the world's Gamay wines. Of this, half is sold simply as Beaujolais ($7 to $10), most of which is fairly insipid. Beaujolais-Villages ($9 to $12), from a smaller, higher elevation area with better drainage, accounts for most high-quality Beaujolais. I have enjoyed many "plain" Beaujolais wines, though, made by serious, committed winemakers, that have tasted far richer and more fruit expressive than pricier Beaujolais-Villages.

Finally, the fattest, most complex Beaujolais wines are known as Cru Beaujolais ($12 to $15), which means they come from one of ten tiny villages, or *crus*. They are Brouilly, Côte de Brouilly, Chénas, Chiroubles, Fleurie, Julienas, Morgon, Moulin-à-Vent, Régnié, and Saint-Amour. Curiously, the word *Beaujolais* is usually absent from Cru Beaujolais wine labels. The producers prefer their wines to be identified by village name alone. Why, I'll never understand.

The balance of the world's Gamay is found mostly in the Loire Valley and Switzerland, where it is usually blended with Pinot Noir to achieve more elegance, though not much. Gamay is also produced in California, with decidedly unhappy results—high alcohol, candied sweetness, and the Sunshine State's legendary lackluster acidity.

 A lightly chilled glass of Beaujolais is a welcome guest at any meal, be it breakfast, lunch, or dinner. That's right, breakfast! Beaujolais, with its light, refreshing mouthfeel, matches seamlessly with omelets and quiches. Try *that* with a Cabernet sometime if you'd like to experience what Conrad meant by "the horror." Beaujolais is the classic picnic partner, the definitive "chillable red" for sandwiches, cold meats, and salads. It is one of the few effective and commonly available choices for dampening the fires of spicy food, thanks to its sweet, ripe fruit, low alcohol, and mouth-cleansing acidity. Mild cheeses, especially those that carry a touch of fruitiness in them, go beautifully with Beaujolais. It is the perfect answer to the oft-asked question "Can I have red wine with that fish?" *Yes!* Beaujolais, with its white-wine–like acidity, light body, and low alcohol, is a good place to start.

TIPS

◆ Since Beaujolais drinks like a white wine, its hallmark high acidity is made more flattering by serving it at a cooler temperature—say, sixty degrees. Stick it in the fridge for thirty minutes or in an ice bucket for ten.

◆ Beaujolais Nouveau, with its hyper-marketed release on the third Thursday of November each year, arrives just in time for Thanksgiving, with its plethora of sweet side dishes. Isn't it fascinating how so much money goes streaming into French coffers as a direct result of the quintessential American holiday of thanks? I'm sure the irony is not lost on our French friends.

◆ Beware! Because Beaujolais Nouveau is, in effect, an unfinished wine, it has a life span of about *six months* in the bottle. So drink up! Wineshops that try to sell you last year's Beaujolais Nouveau, even at $4 a bottle, are run by evil little men.

CABERNET FRANC

Unknown, unloved, unbeatable with food. Throughout my personal odyssey of wine and food experimentation, Cabernet Franc has consistently emerged as unbelievably food-friendly. Its flavors typically run to raspberry, cedar, bell pepper, and herbs.

The downside of Cabernet Franc is that the search for quality examples can be a hellish undertaking. When you do strike gold, you'll probably have found an Anjou Rouge, Saumur-Champigny, Chinon, or Bourgueil from the upper Loire in northwest France (home of juicy Sauvignons like Sancerre and Pouilly-Fumé). Cabernet Franc is the only red variety that can ripen with color and extract in this cool white wine climate. Pinot tries in Sancerre Rouge and Sancerre Rosé but rarely provides more than thin gruel. I have found Loire Cab Franc from merely marginal vintages with good color and reasonable balance. Many a wine lover may wonder at my fondness for this fascinating grape, but I have come to believe that a well-made $10 or $12 Saumur-Champigny—with its medium weight, ripe piquant fruit, and delicate herbal finish—must be, dollar for dollar, the best of all possible red wines for food.

Cabernet Franc is also a major component of Bordeaux in the Merlot-based Pomerol and St.-Emilion wines. When tasting Bordeaux, I usually find that the wines with the greatest length of flavor are those with a good shot of juicy Cabernet Franc in them. Yet it remains a virtually unknown variety to most consumers, even to countless brokers, bankers, and gynecologists from Westchester who gobble up these profound Bordeaux wines as futures, cellar and resell them at auction, and take their profits, yet rarely open and drink a bottle. Heathen bastards.

In northern Italy (Lombardy, just east and north of Piedmont), Cabernet Franc is labeled by its name and producer, and also is the primary component of the fascinating Franciacorta Rosso. Franciacorta is traditionally a blend of Cabernet Franc with small amounts of Barbera and Merlot. Pounce if you find a good one. You'll be lucky if you find any.

The very qualities that generally repel most Cabernet/Merlot sleepwalkers from this fascinating cool-climate variety—its green, herbaceous notes and high acidity—serve to make it sing with many foods, especially those that are oiled, highly acidified (citrus or tomato), or green (vegetables and salads).

Cabernet Franc is the perfect answer to a host of difficult food questions. Need a light red for fish? Serving a vegetable lasagna or a red sauce with lots of fresh basil or other herbs? Cooking up something from a vegetarian cookbook? Anything with chèvre in it? Cab Franc is your grape.

TIPS

◆ Cabernet Franc drinks well in its youth, though it can display fine longevity in St.-Emilion and Pomerol, and in the best wines of the Loire.

◆ As with most American wines, Cabernet Franc from this country usually has the living daylights oaked out of it. Why do they even bother to grow the damned thing? It's actually insulting.

HOUSEKEEPING

STORAGE: DO'S AND DON'TS

Oxygen

Just like the browning over that begins within minutes of cutting open a ripe fruit, wine begins to deteriorate the moment you pull the cork. Short-term exposure to oxygen, commonly known as "breathing time," can actually have a positive effect in opening up the flavor and aromatics of deeply extracted red wines. But this is a matter of minutes or hours only. Terminal oxidation, the dreaded enemy of all wines, occurs because of an ill-fitting or dried-out cork or from prolonged exposure to heat (anything much above 75 degrees Fahrenheit we'll call heat). When a bottle stands upright for months or even years at your local liquor store, the cork, now out of contact with the wine, becomes dry. As the cork dries, it shrinks, oxygen slips in, "good night nurse."

Heat

Wine is most comfortable in the temperature range that people are—make that Eskimo-type people. For short-term storage (less than six months), 65 to 75 degrees should be fine. Longer term, as close to 55 degrees as possible is ideal. What is more important is that wines are extremely discomforted by temperature fluctuation. A constant 65 degrees all year long is preferable to 45 in January and then 75 in July. An unfinished basement in East Meadow is not quite the same as the ancient Roman cellars under the city of Beaune. Expect your wines to mature accordingly.

Humidity

Humidity keeps wine corks supple and expanded. Sixty percent humidity is just about perfect for long-term storage. Less will accelerate cork shrinkage. More, and after a year or so you'll need to hack through a seven-layer cake of moss and lichen to read your wine labels—if they haven't rotted away entirely.

Odors

Once I left a case of Barolo in my mother's laundry room. Years went by. Mom, ever pragmatic, threw an old bath mat over it and used it to set a spell and wait out the final rinse. In 1986, three min-

utes after it dawned on me that I actually owned a case of 1971 Barolo (a killer vintage now approaching otherworldliness), I arrived with "Miss you, Mom! What's for dinner?"

Up the basement steps, dusty Barolo in hand, I climbed, triumphant, Mom's eyes twinkling with pride. Steaming on the table, her infamous Jewish ziti. The cork, the pour, the sniff . . . Wisk! We poured the whole case out and laughed like hell. Later on we shared some port and did a load of whites together. Wine corks are porous.

Light

"Gee, honey, isn't the new wine rack lovely? It's so pretty the way the setting sun streams in the room and makes the bottles all glow like little prisms." "Yeah, dear, they sure look swell."

Four or five sunsets through that dining room window is probably all your wines will need before you might as well toss them right down the sink with my '71 Barolo.

Vibration

Never store wine near a rail line. That nearly imperceptible tingling on the ball of your foot each time the number 3 rolls through will age all hell out of your Bordeaux.

THE BAD BOTTLE

Shipping

Many wines are D.O.A. in the U.S.A. They are shipped from Europe in nonrefrigerated containers virtually all year round by greedy, bottom-line importers who are simply too dim to realize that their product is not iron ore. A few days on a Baltimore dock in July is usually sufficient to strip the bejeezus out of a fine wine. Wines "cooked" in such a way have no personality; they are lifeless and dull.

Look for the telltale signs of mistreatment. Dried or sticky wine residue on or near the cork or its capsule (covering of metal or plastic), oozing down the bottle, and staining the label are all danger

signs. Watch out for corks that have been pushed out even the slightest amount from expansion inside the bottle, usually due to extreme temperature changes. Somewhere in this wine's journey, it has been exposed to heat or freezing conditions. Don't even bother opening such a bottle. Don't buy it, or if you do, return it unopened.

"Corked" Wine

Cork, the bark of a forty-year-old Portuguese tree, was once, of course, a living organism. After being harvested, dried, bleached and sterilized, it is finally rendered inert. But the best I can figure is that sometimes a few of those microscopic critters come alive again. They become . . . *undead!*

When this happens, as it does far too often, the wine is ruined from contact with this now funky piece of bark. Interestingly enough, we say such a wine is *corked,* and it will smell and taste of cork to prove it. What little wine flavor remains will be utterly masked by corkiness. This condition is nobody's fault except the wine industry's for not moving more quickly to replace natural cork with synthetic cork. Even screw caps perform better than corks, el cheapo stigma notwithstanding.

Send a corked wine back in a restaurant or return it to the place you bought it, on the same or the very next day if possible. If you wait too long, the wine will become so oxidized with its own characteristic odor that it may not be recognizable as corked. Come to think of it, why not Vacu-Vin the damn thing (see page 106) so as to preserve its singular offensiveness, just in case you need to prove its undrinkable condition to some wineshop ignat with whom you are not well acquainted. Don't forget to take your Vacu-Vin stopper back.

A classic misconception is that wine corks smell like the wine contained in their bottles. To a nominal extent this may be true. But little information can be gleaned from a wine cork, so please don't ever sniff a wine cork in a public place. Doing so is akin to lighting up a giant neon "shmuck" sign on your forehead. A waiter or a sommelier may do so, however. That's his job. The reason is that with the frequency of cork-spoiled wines, a quick brush under the nose can immediately reveal the acrid, mildew-like rankness of a bad cork. The waiter can ditch the bottle, sparing you and your guests the joy of kicking off a big evening with a mouthful of cork juice.

Winemaker Error

The most common source of bad wine is a muttonhead winemaker.

False Alarms

SEDIMENT

After four or five years, many better red wines begin the process of shedding their tannins. These tannins fall from the wine in the form of sediment—sometimes as a fine silt, others (later on in the wine's evolution) as heavier deposits, more like flakes of solidified red wine. Usually, wines that throw off the most sediment are better wines; they are unfined and unfiltered when they are bottled and so contain more grape solids. In the case of ten- or twenty-year-old vintage port, you may encounter a repulsive sludge-like material resembling something lost by the *Exxon Valdez.* This, too, is a naturally occurring condition. Sedimented wines are cleared by a process called decanting (see next page).

CRUD ON THE CORK

You don't have to be Louis Pasteur to know that mold will form in a damp cellar. That's why wines stored in earthen (mostly European) cellars tend to develop a bit of mold between their corks and their capsules. This is harmless. Simply wipe off the lip of the bottle after opening. If you plan on reinserting this cork, though, do not use the soiled end first. The wine will splash up against it and be ruined. Mold development is rare on American wine corks. Here, climate-controlled warehouses keep everything nice and neat.

DECANTING: WHEN AND HOW

Saturday night. The big dinner party. Your guests, primed with Champagne, eagerly await the meal you've spent the past few days preparing. As the moment of truth approaches, you repair to the kitchen to open the wine. As you do, you recall groveling for advice at the local wineshop and how, at last, the nice man winked and softly purred, "This is the hottest Cabernet in the store." His confidence and that sagelike beard would have sealed the deal—even if you hadn't been utterly desperate.

Now you pull the cork. It's an awfully long one. Now you pour the wine. It's mighty dark. Now you taste. It's tree sap, and you're pissed. The kitchen is warm, your head begins to spin, you feel your knees going. "Honey, is the wine open?" You lean against the refrigerator and think: "Where is that bastard with the beard?" You're suddenly reveling in the anatomical damage that can be wrought by a rage-driven bottle of Cabernet Sauvignon. Snap out of it! Stow your vengeance in the kitchen drawer and listen up.

Chances are the offending wine *is* a great Cabernet—it's just too young to drink. Until its time arrives (five or ten years down the road), you're forced to deal with that snarkiest of vinous vexations—tannin, the element in grape skins that makes a young red feel like sandpaper. These tannins serve to carry the fruit and other components through what should be a long and successful maturation process, one that eventually brings out the subtlety and complexity of a great red wine. But aging curves are small comfort now, with your big dinner party on the ropes in the next room. The only possible salvation in this instance is vigorous aeration; while not capable of transforming a brawny young red wine into a mature masterpiece, it may at least soften its rough tannic edges.

Decanting for Aeration

You will need two widemouthed, liter-size, indestructible bistro carafes—not the delicate crystal from your grandmother's china cabinet. A major California wine producer (who sells no wine before its time) markets his modest product in just such a carafe for about $3 or $4. The "wine" may be gently decanted into the sink; it's the glass you want.

Empty that savage red into one of the carafes. This single action is equivalent to a half hour or so of "breathing." As you stand at the sink and toss the contents back and forth from one carafe to the other, you'll gain an additional five or six minutes of aeration time for each toss. After two or three minutes (around twenty-five tosses), your hard, ungiving red should become appreciably softer—as though it had been aired for several hours.

There is no clear-cut science to all this. Just toss to taste and hope you can coax the wine to where you want it before the roast gets cold. Beyond this, you may take some comfort in the fact that full-flavored foods—fatty meats and birds (steak, lamb, duck), and anything fried or containing eggplant—create a sort of "tannin cushion" in the mouth. These types of foods actually require wines with significant tannic grip to stand up to their oily mouthfeel.

P.S. A few extra turns of the pepper mill over the food also works wonders in muting tannins.

Decanting for Sediment

Sediment is a good sign in wines that are built for long-term aging. Great Bordeaux and Burgundy, big Rhône wines, and better Cabernets, as well as Barolos, Brunellos, and their kin, will all throw serious sediments. You will need to know how to separate out this aesthetically distracting (and gritty feeling) flotsam. Welcome to the world of decanting. Although this appears as mysterious as voodoo to the novice oenophile, the decanting process is a piece of cake. Be confident.

The critical first step is to stand the bottle upright for several hours or even days to allow the sediment to settle at the bottom of the bottle. Now remove the entire capsule from the neck for better visibility. Hold a flashlight or the flame of a candle (more romantic) just behind the bottle's neck to illuminate the flow. In one slow, steady motion, pour the wine into a clean decanter (your grandmother's crystal?), never righting the bottle until the silt-like material has reached the neck or upper shoulder of the bottle (almost the end of the wine). You should be able to stop pouring just before remixing the sediment with the now clear wine.

The last half inch of wine and sediment can be poured down the drain, or it can be strained through a coffee filter. You may ask, "Why not simply pour the whole damn thing through a filter in the first place and be done with it?" Wine filtered in this manner will be stripped of flavor nuance, so don't be lazy.

If you prefer to serve the decanted wine in its original bottle, rinse it with cool water and refill it from the decanter with a funnel (plastic only).

IS OLDER WINE BETTER?

The idea that old wine is invariably better than young is misleading. Significant aging should really apply only to a narrow range of wines—rarely to the kind you depend on throughout the year.

Powerful red wines from unusually fine vintage years can gain considerably in aromatic and flavor complexity as they age—up to a point, that is. These prize examples of the winemaker's art are the wines you read about at big-time tasting events. These are the wines that well-heeled enthusiasts and collectors seek out, taste, and discuss ad nauseam. The wines that fall into this category are almost exclusively the great châteaux red wines of Bordeaux. Other ageable reds include red Burgundies and tarry, opulent Barolos and Brunellos from Italy. High-end California Cabernets and other big, tannic reds from around the world also appreciate qualitatively in bottle for periods of anywhere from ten years to as many as twenty years or more in very special cases. Other less expensive red wines may benefit from an additional two to five years of bottle age. But even these are exceptions.

Age alone is no assurance of quality and is more often a sign of exhaustion. The fact that a wine can make it to an old age does not guarantee that it will be a "ripe" old age. The overwhelming majority of everyday wines (under $15 a bottle, let's say) are ready to drink when they are released, often as young as a year or two, and have a serviceable life span of three to four years at best.

As for whites, aside from a handful of top-notch Burgundies, Loire Chenin Blancs, Austrian Gruners, and better German, Alsatian, and Austrian Rieslings (which in great vintages can gain complexity for as long as twenty years), white wines should be drunk up as young as you can find them. Their mouthwatering freshness fades, and as it does, they become dull and lifeless. Usually, when a white wine's third birthday rolls around, it should be drunk up. Actually, most of the world's lightest, juiciest, most refreshing white wines (e.g., Italian whites, Muscadet from the Loire, and Sauvignons from Bergerac) are never more mouthwateringly delicious than within their first year and a half of life.

A wine that has passed its peak and is losing fruit and acidity has begun an irreversible slide into palookaville. At retail and in many restaurants, such a wine is known as a "closeout," wholesaled cheaply for speedy depletion and maximum retail profit— and, frankly, lusted for by greedy retailers, restaurateurs, and bargain-obsessed consumers. A dull dried-out wine is never a bargain.

SERVING TEMPERATURE

Reds

It is remarkable that even people with serious wine savvy give little or no thought to how to present wines to their best advantage. Red wines are generally served directly from where they lie at whatever the room temperature of the moment may be, usually somewhere between 70 and 116 degrees. Warm temperatures, like those produced in the wine rack on top of your refrigerator, volatilize the alcohol in a wine to a level so exaggerated as to mask and nearly obliterate all flavor and aromatic nuance. Most red wines are far more flatteringly presented at just 10 degrees or so above cellar temperature, say at about 65 or 70 degrees.

Now, if you lack that cool, mossy cellar to send Jeeves scurrying off to just before dinner, the simplest way to achieve optimal serving temperature for red wines is to place them in your refrigerator thirty minutes before mealtime. This should lower the wine's temperature the 10 degrees or so necessary for peak drinkability. Beaujolais and other high-acid, chillable reds get an additional fifteen to thirty minutes, as serving them cooler helps to mollify their characteristic high acid. These great, food-friendly red wines actually behave much like whites, you see. And if you go too far, waiting a few minutes for a slightly over-chilled red wine to warm up a bit is far preferable to being stuck with a hot, unbalanced red.

Whites

We tend to serve white and sparkling wines as if they were soda. Straight from the refrigerator, typically at somewhere around 35 degrees, is okay for simple and rustic whites without much character. At this frigid temperature, though, the bouquet and flavor of opulent white wines remain closed and remote. In any case, drinking better whites and Champagnes straight from the fridge is a sure bet for a lost opportunity, since you can be assured that nothing of interest will get through.

IS THAT A WOOLLY MAMMOTH IN THERE?

The question is often asked, "How long may I safely keep a bottle of white wine or Champagne on ice?" Wines that languish in the refrigerator for much longer than six to eight weeks begin to lose flavor and aromatic impact. Wines so trapped in this frosty embrace begin a slow, yet inevitable decline into vinous cryogenia. You don't want to go there. As for Champagne, many people tell me they have a bottle in their refrigerator that they've been saving since 1956 for a special occasion. Well, sooner or later, there'll be a funeral: yours.

So, the technique for serving temperature is simple enough. Cool down room-temperature reds and allow fine whites and Champagnes an opportunity to strut their stuff.

THE GRIP—A TIP

The bowl of a wineglass is an extremely effective conductor of heat. Clocking in at around 98.6 degrees Fahrenheit, your handling it will crank up a wine's temperature to an unpleasant level lickety-split. In addition, let's face it: We humans are a greasy species, so for God's sake keep your hot, sweaty mitts off the bowl of your wineglass. Always hold a wineglass by the stem or the base. Not only will you enjoy the wine at its most flattering temperature, your glass will also remain neat and free of fingerprints—and, frankly, the right wineglass grip shows terrific breeding.

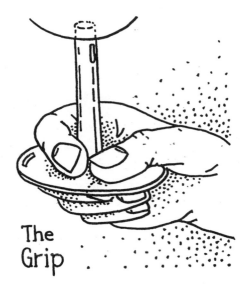

The
Grip

THE SULFITE THING

Since time immemorial, tiny amounts of sulfur have been used in the winemaking process to retard development of undesirable microorganisms, prevent oxidation, and inhibit the growth of wild yeasts and bacteria. White wines, which are less stable than reds, are generally sulfured more heavily and sometimes possess a burnt-match aroma when first opened. This scent can blow off after several minutes. In heavily dosed examples, it is simply a result of ruinous winemaking.

For most people, the presence of sulfites in wine is a nonissue. We're talking about 20 or 30 parts per million. The dietary signifi-cance for people who are allergic to sulfur applies to perhaps only

105

1 in 10,000, and most of these sulfur-sensitive consumers are aware that they must avoid wine because of the inclusion of this generally benign substance.

The infamous *Sulfite Warning* label on all wine bottles sold in the U.S. represents merely the latest lobbying efforts by America's hysterical neo-Prohibitionists—yet another humiliating blow to culinary civility.

Unless you are allergic to sulfur dioxide, its presence in wine is *not* a cause of headaches. Headaches and hangovers are invariably caused by any combination of:

- how allergen-sensitive you are in general, especially toward histamines, which are a natural component of red wines
- how much food is in your stomach
- how much sleep you didn't get the night before
- how much water you've consumed during the evening (a lot is better)
- how big of a pig you've been at the trough

Consumers often link "organic" wines with "nonsulfite" wines. This is a big mistake. They are not the same. While I endorse the practice of organic vineyard cultivation (no synthetic pesticides or fertilizers), the use of sulfites in preserving a wine's stability is an essential part of winemaking. Most organic wines are treated with sulfites, just as nonorganic wines are.

SAVING OPENED WINE

As I mentioned in the chapter on storage, once you open a bottle of wine, exposure to oxygen begins an inexorable process of deterioration. Whereas the life expectancy of an opened bottle of wine ranges anywhere from twenty minutes to twelve hours, most wines begin to fall apart in just a few hours. Oxygen is the enemy of opened wine and must be kept out at all costs. Fortunately, the cost of accomplishing this is only around $15.

The gadget is called Vacu-Vin. (This is the proprietary name of a single brand of this type of wine preservation pump; there are other makers.) This pocket-sized miracle is a hand-operated vacuum pump with a one-way bleeder valve that evacuates air from an open bottle with a rubber stopper that substitutes for the wine's cork. The result is opened wine that retains a high degree of freshness for as long as a week.

Vacu-Vin was invented by an unsung Dutch visionary named Bernd Schneider and represents a technological breakthrough akin to the invention of the electric toaster and baseball games at night. The device opens up new vistas of opportunity for restaurants and consumers, now freed from the need to consume or sacrifice the balance of a full bottle of wine at one sitting. Vacu-Vin means that we can now open a half-dozen or more wines for guests to taste at a dinner party, restaurants can safely offer vast numbers of wine by the glass, and consumers everywhere can match specific wines and foods with newfound élan.

The fastest way for you to become wildly successful at marrying wine and food is to open three or four bottles, all from differ-

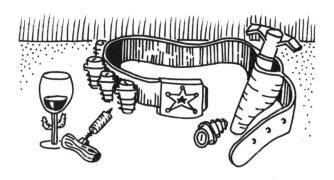

ent grape varieties, at your big family meal on Saturday or Sunday evening. Try each of the four wines with whatever you're serving, Vacu-Vin them up, and try the same four wines with whatever you cook or bring in each night the rest of the week. This will allow you to experience for yourself which varieties have the most versatile food applications and which have the least.

There is absolutely no reason why any civilized human should not own a Vacu-Vin and a dozen stoppers. Get with it!

TIPS

◆ A terrific way of saving extra wine in an oxygen-free environment is to pour off half of a newly opened full bottle into a clean, empty half-bottle and immediately stopper it with a cork. A half-bottle preserved in this way is the most effective method for keeping wine fresh, even better than Vacu-Vin.

COOKING WITH WINE

Never put anything in your food that you wouldn't put in your mouth. Wine is an integral part of fine cooking and, as such, should not be a mere afterthought. Adding it together with the aromatic vegetables and herbs that are sautéed early on concentrates its flavor and helps form the foundation of any great sauce, soup, or stew. Since all alcohol burns off in the first eight to ten minutes of cooking, it's the acidity and flavor in a wine that count. A well-made wine, albeit an inexpensive one, is what's needed. On the other hand, for the lousy half-cup or so that a typical recipe calls for, why not live it up a bit? Try reducing a few ounces of that $30 Bordeaux or Cabernet and folding it into your sauce base. Then you can name the dish after the wine and feel as rich as Croesus.

White Wines

You want wines with high acidity, the more character the better, and absolutely no oak. Use Trebbiano, inexpensive Sauvignon Blanc and white Bordeaux, Gascony whites, and any California jug wine with 11% or more alcohol (higher alcohol ensures less sweetness).

Red Wines

You want wines with earthy flavors and light to medium body, especially in the case of reductions, where a rich, tannic wine can become bitter. Lighter, fruitier wines like Pinot Noir, inexpensive Montepulciano d'Abruzzo, or Beaujolais are good choices for most cooking purposes.

TIPS

- ◆ Tomato-based sauces: add high-acid reds like Barbera, Cabernet Franc, Pinot Noir, Gamay, or Sangiovese.
- ◆ Many cooks keep leftover or spoiled wine in the kitchen cabinet for eventual "cooking" purposes. "Feh!" I say. Leftover and spoiled wine should be poured down the sink with other culinary flotsam.

Retail

Buyer Beware

There is no more significant action you can take to change your life, short of dying, than that of locating an enlightened wineshop. The wine retailer is your one indispensable source for interesting, small-production, food-friendly wines, and his importance cannot be overemphasized. You'll find only mediocrity at the local grocery.

BAD OMENS

Remember, wine is a living entity. It is the product of crushed grapes, protected only by being closeted away from the elements—temperature extremes, air, and light.

Heat

If you feel the need to take your coat off when you walk into a wine store, keep it on, turn around, and keep walking. You can leave and go home, but the wines have to stay and sweat it out. Temperatures warm enough to hang out in your underwear are bad news for wine. A warm wineshop should make you plenty nervous. A wineshop cannot be too cool.

Most wine and liquor stores in cities at least tend to lie on major avenues at the street level of large apartment buildings. The huge furnaces that fire these buildings and the pipes that deliver hot water to them often lie mighty close to the cellars and the actual selling floor of these shops. They can raise the temperature dangerously high for even the short-term health of fine wines. Touch your hands to the bottles. Do they feel cool, as they should, or warm?

Fluorescent Lights

Every store has them, right? Wrong. Most do, and even brief exposure to them beats the hell out of wine. (Did you know that fluorescent light fades watercolor paintings right on the wall?)

Standing Stock

When wines stand upright for long periods, corks that are out of contact with wine dry, shrink, and allow air to enter. This can happen quickly, in only a few months, in a warm environment. Unless they're rapid-turnover wines, they are at risk of spoilage.

HOW TO CHOOSE A GOOD WINESHOP

Take stock of the stock:

- ◆ Is anyone in charge present regularly (an owner or manager)?
- ◆ Does the inventory appear to be treated with respect, or do you see torn labels and dusty bottles everywhere?
- ◆ Are wines organized by region, grape types, or even color (whites in one area, reds in another), or are bottles scattered everywhere with no seeming rhyme or reason?

- ◆ Are there old white wines in the store (four years or more)? *Exceptions: Loire Chenin Blanc wines, German and Alsace Rieslings, Chablis, and better white Burgundies from great vintages.*
- ◆ Cut cases and bin stackings: This is the profit engine of most wineshops. Bins account for up to 30% of retailers' business, and naturally they like to load them up with wines whose primary attribute is a healthy markup. What appears to be a bargain at $6 or $7 is often a poorly made $5 wine. Its position in the sweet spot of the selling floor ensures high turnover and profit. Unless you know a wineshop well, avoid cut cases and bin stackings.

Take stock of the staff:

A pretty label does not mean a good wine. Nor does a witty "shelf talker." Is there anyone offering assistance? If so, don't be shy; ask for a recommendation. A good wine merchant has tasted most of his inventory and can communicate—in a language you can understand—about wine. If he cannot, shop somewhere else. Of course, pay scale in wineshops being what it is (or isn't), don't expect to be waited on by the world's greatest wine authority. It does happen, but not often. Hope, at least, for someone who seems sincerely passionate about the subject. Be wary of sales help or management who claim "all wines go with everything." They don't!

The Interview—a few key questions for wineshop personnel or management:

Do you have any Cabernet Franc? (Does he know that Chinon, Bourgueil, and Saumur-Champigny are made from Cabernet Franc?)

Do you have any reds from Calabria or Apulia? Do you know where these places are in Italy (the "toe" and the "heel")? Do you know where Italy is?

Where's the Pinot? (Does he immediately know you mean Pinot Noir?)

Do you have any *grower* Champagne (small-production, non-mass-market Champagne)?

What's on the Shelf?

A bigger selection is not a better selection. How many Chardonnays, Cabernets, and Merlots a wineshop carries in inventory is not an indicator of quality, nor is it an inspiration for your food/wine needs. On the next page is a short list of wines that should quicken the pulse of consumers searching for a superior wine retailer.

SPARKLING WINES

Prosecco

Cremant d'Alsace

Riesling Sekt or sparkling Chenin Blanc (Vouvray or Montlouis)

Five Champagnes you have never heard of, none with C.M. or M.A. in tiny letters at the bottom of the label (see Champagne chapter)

WHITE WINES

Loire Chenin Blancs (two or three Vouvrays and a Savennières)

Rieslings (5 = why bother?   10 = poor   15 = fair   20 = good   25 = rock 'n' roll   30+ = Valhalla)

Alsace wines (two or three each of Pinot Blancs, Gewürztraminers, Rieslings, and Tokays)

New Zealand Sauvignon Blancs (three at least—all nonoaked)

Albarinos from Spain (one or two, very fresh)

Gruner Veltliners from Austria (one or two)

RED WINES

Pinot Noirs (American Pinots and French Burgundies combined, fifteen at least)

Cabernet Francs (Loire—Chinon, Bourgueil, Saumur-Champigny; Cabernet Franc or Franciacorta Rosso from northern Italy. Three or more of the above would be lovely.)

Barbera from Italy (two or three)

SHOPPING ROUTINE:
Convenience Versus Quality

Where do you shop for wine? The most common answer is just down the street or around the corner. Let's face it: Wine bottles are heavy. Walking even a block or two out of the way with fingers clutching your briefcase, groceries, dry cleaning, and other assorted minutiae can be just too much to bear. So you briefly stop and grab a bottle of something, and you're on your way. Chances are the wine came out of the sale bin and is as unexciting as everything else in a typical store, but you figure, "Well, I guess that's the way wine tastes."

Know this! As a source of high-quality, high-value wines, the overwhelming majority of wineshops, outlets, and groceries are pathetic. Like great wines, there are very few great wineshops, but you'd be nuts not to seek one out. When you find one, better quality will show in every wine you buy, no matter the price point.

A New Shopping Technique

Try this. *Change wineshops!* Instead of settling for the same old plonk from the same old place, make a pilgrimage once or twice a month to that über-shop across town. Put together an assorted case or two, and have it delivered. (Oftentimes, there's a case discount, you know.) Whether you're whipping up something special in the kitchen or just ordering in, you'll have choice! You're not locked in to the one or two bottles you happen to have lying around. You can choose the exact wine you want with dinner. Now you can have five chilled whites and a bottle of Prosecco awaiting your every whim. Now you can live like a civilized human. "Top of the food chain, Ma!"

WINE IN
RESTAURANTS
Dining's Downside

MARKUP: THOSE BASTARDS!

$\mathcal{A}$ simple Chardonnay or Merlot from the south of France will typically sell on a New York City wine list for somewhere between $20 and $24. The wholesale cost to the restaurant is $4. You don't need a master's in business to see that this generates a 500 to 600 percent profit. And while a more expensive wine, like a Châteauneuf du Pape or a decent Napa Cabernet that wholesales at $15, may be ratcheted up only 300 percent, to $45, that's still a $30 profit for simply pulling a cork and pouring four glasses of wine. If restaurants marked up food the way they do wine, we'd all be eating at home every night and asking, "What's a Zagat?"

Many restaurateurs, and I use the term loosely, consider the wine side of the house their best crack at subsidizing their rents and so attempt to wring every penny they can from it. Restaurants that insult consumers by gouging on wine prices should be avoided.

The outrageous markups routinely inflicted on wine drinkers make it difficult for them to find affordable wines for their restaurant meals, deter them from experimenting with non-mass-market varieties or lesser-known producers, and go far in explaining why the enjoyment of wine and food in this country is perceived as an elitist pursuit.

AUTHOR! AUTHOR!

Once I wrote a small wine list for a hot New York City trattoria. I was "instructed" by the owner (a humble man and a fine human being) to price a Chianti wholesaling at $3.50 at $28. Thank heaven I didn't have to sign the bloody thing. A few weeks later, I sat down and opened the list in a critically acclaimed Manhattan restaurant to find a desultory mishmash of wildly overpriced second- and third-rate losers from all over the globe, laid out with no particular rhyme or reason. Could one person have intentionally assembled this nightmare? Yup. There at the bottom, the palate-dead homunculus himself had actually signed his name under the stunning misnomer *Wine Director*. Help!

Who writes these wine lists, you may wonder. Assembling a restaurant's wine list is a job that may be handed off to a general manager, the headwaiter, a bartender, or the boss's wife—if it isn't dispatched to some hack salesman from a local liquor wholesaler who promises to "take care of the printing costs." In any case, whoever winds up with the job, he loves it primarily for one reason: ego pump. Whether knowledgeable on the subject of wine or not, the wine salesman's dogged pursuit and the endless phone chitchat are a blissful way of killing time and feeling important. What's more maddening still is that even many chefs (who you would assume would be terrific at choosing wine) have no idea whatsoever what a good wine should taste like or the foggiest notion of which wines will actually complement their food. That is why a legitimately well chosen wine list, whether numbering a dozen wines or a hundred, is nearly impossible to find.

THE SCORECARD

A Good Wine List Has . . .

- 15 percent or more of the list priced under $20
- nonoaked Sauvignon Blancs (French, New Zealand, South African)
- German and Alsace whites (Riesling, Pinot Blanc, Tokay Pinot Gris, Gewürztraminer)
- Vouvray (or other Chenin Blanc wine from the Loire)
- Sparkling Prosecco
- Light reds: Beaujolais, Pinot Noir, Barbera, and Cabernet Franc wines, etc.
- By the glass: five or more whites, five or more reds, one sparkler, and a dessert wine
- Wine/food pairing suggestions for specific wines targeted to individual dishes (printed or orally offered)

A Bad Wine List Has . . .

- A ridiculous preponderance of oak-bludgeoned Chardonnays and Sauvignon Blancs (American, Australian, Chilean, whatever)
- Any of the following wines priced much over $20: Beaujolais, Pinot Grigio from the Veneto, Chardonnay or Merlot *vin de pays* from southwest France, anything from Chile
- Wines listed without producers' names
- Lotsa nationally advertised brands

HOW TO FIND A GOOD WINE ON A LOUSY LIST

Often, the best option on a poor wine list isn't even on the wine list. It's the lowly house wine. If they're pouring those 1.5-liter jug wines, Trebbiano or Montepulciano d'Abruzzo from Italy, or ubiquitous French zip code blanc de blancs and cuvées rouges, you're in luck. They are always fresh, light, and blissfully nonoaked, which makes a fine, light accompaniment to most foods. Like good physicians, they "do no harm," as in smothering subtle food flavors with overextraction, high alcohol, and oaky residues. At $4 or $5 a glass, drink up.

RESTAURANT ETIQUETTE

The Cork

If some waitron in an apron presents you with a wine cork as if it were the Klopman Diamond, just say, "Oh, thanks, you can keep that." Sniffing, squeezing, or otherwise fondling a wine cork is a sure sign you hail from an alternate universe.

Holding a Wineglass Up to the Light

Only a total meniscus looks for color or clarity or legs or sheets or some such pretentious folderol. If you feel you must, peering through the wine at a white tablecloth or napkin will supply all needed visual data, including color and clarity. (By the way, a luscious, unfiltered Pinot Noir or a bestial red Dao from Portugal will rarely be crystal clear. So don't get carried away with the clarity issue.)

Not Tasting (For the Truly Hip)

In most cases, the quasi-religious ritual of tasting a wine for approval is irrelevant. A quick sniff should suffice if you know what you're looking for, be it the clean freshness of new Muscadet or the manure-pile reek of a good Côtes de Roussillon. If a wine smells right, or at least like wine, wave the waiter to get on with it. You'll look totally cool, and probably get a tad more attention from your waiter for the balance of the evening.

He Who Serves— What Do You Call That Guy?

A *sommelier* is a person who manages the wine list, advises on food and wine pairings, and serves wine full-time in the few restaurants that can afford to employ such a person. Do yourself a favor: Don't ask to see the *wine steward* unless you're on the *QE2*. Stewards work on boats.

Returning a Wine

Far too often, bad corks make their presence known by reacting with a wine, flattening out the wine's aroma and replacing it with one redolent of cork. If a wine smells like cork, you should inform the waiter that it's "corked" and refuse it. A wine should also be returned if it is inappropriately cloudy, has a chemical odor, smells madeirized (like sherry), or is vinegary or vegetal—like when you lift the lid off the pot you steamed broccoli in two nights ago. If a wine is simply made from an exotic grape variety you have yet to experience (as in *not* Chardonnay, Cabernet, or Merlot), give it a chance. Have a glass. Wonders may await.

RESTAURANT NOTICES

(That Really Mean "We're Outta Here")

◆ CLOSED FOR RENOVATIONS

◆ CLOSED FOR KITCHEN FIRE

◆ CLOSED TWO WEEKS FOR VACATION (IN DECEMBER)

◆ CLOSED—WILL REOPEN UNDER NEW MANAGEMENT

◆ CLOSED—STOVE BROKE

An Open Letter to Restaurant Critics

$\mathcal{A}$ s a consumer, I find that the quest for good, fairly priced wines on restaurant wine lists is that of a lonely pilgrim speaking in a language that few understand. Our most influential guide should be the restaurant reviewer. Writers who never mention wine in their reviews should be flogged, or banished to the obituary page. Many who do give ink to the wine list generally dismiss this duty with vapid phrases like "The wine list at the Carnage House is small but well chosen" or ". . . has all the big names but at high prices." As for mention of specific wines: "An appealing Merlot from Sneer Valley Vineyards was a good choice at $38." *Thirty-eight dollars?* For $38, you should be able to buy two glasses of Champagne and a bottle of Beaujolais with your dinner. Critics, have you no inkling what a restaurant pays for wine?

"The Pinot Blanc of Karl Zitz at $27 goes quite nicely with this food." That Alsace Pinot Blanc, though perhaps a smart little wine, cost the restaurateur $6 a bottle. That's a $21 gross profit, or a whopping 450 percent markup. A price of $18 or $20 would be more appropriate. Critics, have your paper spring for a subscription to the local *Beverage Media* (the wine and liquor industry wholesale bible) and find out what restaurants pay for wine. Then begin to review wine list pricing realistically. You'll have lots of fun with this, as scandalous price gouging abounds. As it is, you are unwitting accomplices to greedy restaurateurs fleecing those customers who merely wish to enjoy a glass at a fair price with a restaurant meal.

The restaurant experience is often the defining moment in the kindling of one's relationship with wine and food, as well as the definitive ideal of what civilized dining should be. Critics, wine is important. Get with it. Put on your wig or your mustache and take a wine class. No one will know. (And I won't tell.)

Bring Your Own

The noble destiny of wine is food. Unfortunately, you must face the fact that even the best restaurants in America often have lousy wine lists. What you like to drink with food is probably not the same as what typical restaurateurs are usually offering.

For foodies, one of the most galling experiences is to unfold an excellent restaurant's wine list and find nothing worth drinking. However, with a deft combination of bluster, finagling, and economic incentive, you too can drink your favorite wines even at vinously challenged restaurants. Here's the drill.

Since a restaurant relies heavily on the profit from its wine list, you should emphasize your willingness to pay whatever "corkage fee" is the policy of the house. This fee can vary wildly. Sometimes it's a standard dollar amount—say, $10 or $20. Other times the waiter asks the owner, the owner sizes you and your wine up, and a sentence is handed down—as in, "What do they have there, Champagne? Charge 'em $25."

That's the way it shakes out when you stroll in with your bottle unannounced. Better to locate the boss on the way out the door one evening, dish him a compliment on the meal, and then call ahead next time with your finely honed script before you. "Hello, André? This is George Metesky. You know, I've enjoyed dining at your restaurant so many times that you immediately came to mind for my dear cousin's investiture next Thursday. Since it's a special occasion, I'd very much appreciate it if we could bring a bottle of the 1970 Château Linch-Pin, a wine from my dear cousin's birth year. Of course, I'm happy to pay whatever corkage fee you might ask, and I'm hoping you'll join us for a glass."

You'd be surprised how often such an approach can work when accompanied by just a little finesse. A good B.Y.O.B. technique can result in a memorable gustatory experience. Again, the keys to the Bring Your Own Bottle phone call are:

1. Identify yourself as a regular customer.
2. Insert flattery.
3. Mention your willingness to pay a corkage fee.
4. Offer André a glass.
5. Avoid any temptation to bring a mediocre or commonly available wine.
6. Never, ever bring anything already offered on the wine list.

WINE RATINGS
What's the Real Score?

MAGAZINES

The popularity of wine magazines is largely due to the public's lack of wine-buying confidence. The very idea of having to purchase a bottle is fraught with terror. We're frightened that we know too little, frightened about the subject being vast, and most of all, frightened by the ultimate faux pas—*buying the wrong wine!*

So we cleave to any quasi-official taster or committee to give us the okay before we dare enter the marketplace and buy. Wine magazines give the illusion of providing this sort of public service. But remember, wine magazines are *not* a public service, like the phone book or the Better Business Bureau. They are, rather, advertiser-financed, profit-making enterprises. As such, they have developed a highly specific, economically driven game plan.

Strictly Averaged

The scoring process itself at this type of "wine lifestyle" magazine is inherently flawed in that it is executed by a *panel of tasters* (anywhere from four to a dozen knuckleheads of questionable vinous pedigree). So a typical assortment of opinions on a given wine, running the gamut from ambrosial to execrable, are lumped together to form a review.

Result: ". . . a well-made, appealing wine of medium body, nice ripeness, and reasonable length of flavor."

Translation: An irrelevant, meaningless description of a wine provided by *averaging out* the divergent opinions of an assortment of tasters.

As nettlesome as this watering down of quality assessment is, a friend of mine, recently charged with distilling judges' notes into actual reviews at a major wine mag, claims he was explicitly instructed (are you sitting down?) to "never, ever say anything negative about any wine." Sweet Jesus! I can only assume this policy is cultivated because wineries are routinely charged entry fees in order to qualify for scoring and awards, and if negatively reviewed, will be reluctant to continue entering their wines—or advertising them.

About Notes

In this type of wine publication, news of the wine world can be interesting, timely, and of real value, but the concept of tasting notes and numerical scoring is problematic at best. For one thing, how many different descriptions can be written about 423 California Chardonnays? Probably three. Here they are:

1. Chardonnay Plywood Cellars 1998 (Carneros)
   Flamboyantly constructed, with gobs of silky, ripe, orchard fruit in an oak-redolent frame. A full-throttle style from this outstanding producer. Drink now or hold until 2012.

2. Chardonnay Creek Stream Vintner's Select 1998 (Sonoma)
   Delicately structured, with mild flavors and a lean, somewhat reticent fruit profile. Finishes with a faint nip of wood tannin, and a quizzical pear-like nuance. Only 83,700 cases produced! Drink in the next five weeks.

3. Chardonnay "Dengue Vineyard" Reserve Lot 3 Cuvée Louise
   Shmenge 1998 (Napa)
   Clearly in the Burgundian style, with oodles of toasty new
   oak flavors and an opulent, clove-scented middle mouthfeel.
   Better now than later.

COUNTY FAIRS AND WINE EXPOS

These marathon, self-serving ego fests provide local palate-dead wine geeks with their biannual fifteen minutes of notoriety. Typically, these *volunteer judges* luge through 300 wines in an afternoon, literally racing one another to see who can finish first and then pass out in their Chicken Cordon Bleu. Naturally, the medals awarded at these events represent genuine merit.

INDIVIDUALLY PENNED NEWSLETTERS

With newsletters authored by a single taster, at least the buck stops with one guy. Basically, you get a sense of his palate, and you agree or you don't. Or you take his opinion on certain wine categories with a grain (or a shaker) of salt. Since most newsletters are subscriber-funded and hence do not rely on advertising, the rating process is invariably more objective than a magazine's. Each newsletter represents the life work of a "nonbiased" taster, and that taster is likely to have a wider experience of wines, both known and obscure, than the average wine magazine editor.

HAVOC

"Wine lifestyle" magazines and newsletters both fulfill a legitimate need but are unfortunately relied on to excess. The leviathan influence of a handful of major wine publications turns most wine buyers into "by-the-number zombies," unable or unwilling to develop authentic judgments on their own. They flock to wine stores, clutching the latest reviews, rabidly seeking the winners. Retailers tell me they can't sell a wine unless it's 90 points, and if it's 90 points, they can't buy it. A classic case of an industry consumed by its own hype.

THE WINE SALESMAN

WINE WRITERS

It is, of course, a delicate business to criticize others in the wine trade when one needs to deal with them on a frequent basis. Wine writers, including many who are read regularly by thousands in major periodicals, can be highly qualified writers indeed. Some are even quite skilled at writing on the subject of wine. But I must confess I have known precious few who have the slightest inkling of how the whole descriptive process relates to food. As for wine writer objectivity, have you ever read a bad review of a mass-market Champagne?

It's been said that a wine writer lives on the smell of an oily rag. The pay is poor, the fame is meager, and you don't really get a lotta babes. On the plus side, the hours are nice, the tastings are catered, and the occasional junket to Sydney or Seville is nothing to sneeze at. Best of all, the samples never stop coming.

THE ANATOMY OF SCORING

The whole business of wine scoring is actually totally incompatible with wine's ultimate, essential purpose—that of serving as a complement to food. The biggest, flashiest, most intensely extracted, high-alcohol monsters are invariably the highest-scoring, award-winning, and most celebrated wines. And of course, they serve as wonderful food partners—as long as you plan on serving Wild Boar with Hunter Sauce next Tuesday night. Back in the real world, it's the simple $7 Beaujolais or Côtes du Rhône that's perfect with carry-out chicken or the countless other casual, uncomplicated foods that we enjoy every day.

Remember, even if wine critics could somehow quantify quality, they could never quantify taste. Your best wine adviser will always remain you, with the assistance of a wine merchant who can prove himself to you. Find one.

CHAMPAGNE
With Respect

If the day ever comes when I am forever banished to the loneliest, most barren wilderness, and I'm asked to choose one wine to drink for the rest of my days, I'll surely say, "Champagne, please." Champagne (the real item, from France) is the most refreshing, elegant, and eminently drinkable of all wines. Its power to stimulate the gastric juices and to cleanse the palate is remarkable. As an apéritif, it has a crisp acidity, a lightness, and an impeccable balance that serve to sharpen the appetite, and the wits, as nothing else can. Its very sound thrills.

Sadly, beneath the great celebration of life that is Champagne, there lurks an ugly secret. The overwhelming bulk of Champagne sold throughout the world, which is produced by a half-dozen mass-market companies, is just plain crap. It's not that these producers set out to make poor wine, or that they are inept. By and large, they are simply incapable of producing anything better in the massive quantities required to meet their market demands. Most of the famous brands are the greatest underachievers. Meanwhile, the small artisanal producers, whose wines you are not likely to encounter at the corner store, offer Champagnes so far above and beyond the big guys in quality as to be like some other beverage entirely. The difference, when the wines are judged side by side, can be breathtaking.

WHERE

The region of Champagne, 90 miles northeast of Paris, provides a fixed amount of high-quality Chardonnay, Pinot Noir, and Pinot Meunier grapes, the only varieties allowed. Most megahouses can't possibly grow or purchase enough of this first-class fruit to meet their huge demands without working on shorter margins or pushing brands out of their price points. So they make do with something less. The resulting wines are often thin and charmless; devoid of character, balance, and flavor; and topped off with just enough sugar to blur the quality baseline.

Why do six Champagne houses control 85 percent of all Champagne business done in the United States? Simply put—marketing. Name recognition is all in the American marketplace. Most folks drink Champagne rarely, if ever. They have absolutely no idea what the real thing is supposed to taste like, and frankly, after a few glasses, who can tell the difference anyway? So on the odd occasion they need to shell out $25 or $30 for a bottle of Champagne, can you realistically expect them to step up to the counter and ask, "Do you have any Guy Larmandier?"

THE TASTE OF CHAMPAGNE

Champagne should have tiny, persistent bubbles. This translates texturally into a creamy mouthfeel. No single element of the Champagne experience is more important. Although flavors can run the gamut from delicate, citrusy apéritif-style up through far richer, more pungent, nearly malty versions, a swallow of well-made Champagne should always leave your mouth feeling refreshed. Its finish should be absolutely clean.

Poorly made Champagne will lack that tightly knit, creamy sensation. Its mouthfeel will seem foamy, flabby, or flat. Lesser Champagnes nearly always carry a filthy, cloying finish. Have a sip, count to ten, smack your lips, and draw in some air. This is the moment of truth. Trust your instincts and your own good taste. When you evaluate the finish of a Champagne this way, poor examples have nowhere to hide. Be confident. If your Champagne fails the test, marinate some fruit in it and try another brand. Get tough!

BREAKING THE CODE

At the bottom edge of every Champagne label, there appear two tiny letters (abbreviations) preceding a six-digit license number. There are four possible pairs of these letters that by French law must appear on every bottle of Champagne. These two letters can open a fascinating window to the inner workings of the world of Champagne.

N.M. (Negociant-Manipulant): A "dealer/producer" who may own vineyards but generally purchases most of its grapes. This producer then creates and markets Champagne under its own label. This category contains the majority of Champagne firms, and so represents the widest range of quality levels. *All* the mass-market Champagnes are Negociant-Manipulant houses. This is not to say that only mediocre Champagne is produced by N.M. firms, but virtually all the Champagne brands you are familiar with are N.M. Though at times very fine, and often exemplary, N.M. wines you'll find in the U.S. market are rarely special.

Quality: Excellent to pathetic.

C.M. (Cooperative-Manipulant): A "co-op/producer." Approximately 11,000 growers pool their resources to produce and market their own Champagne brands. There are 150 such firms.

Quality: Decent to poor.

M.A. (Marque d'Acheteur): Buyer's own brand. He owns no vineyards and makes no Champagne. He buys Champagne from growers, co-ops, or negociants and markets them under various labels. You too can import your very own Champagne with your very own label. How about "Beatrice Brut Reserve"? This would be accomplished by engaging a broker to purchase a pre-made wine for your label. There's a catch, though. A first shipment may be of potable quality, but that of succeeding batches can vary wildly. An M.A. Champagne will always be the cheapest Champagne on the shelf at the wineshop, and with good reason.

Quality: Occasionally Champagne-like; more often, execrable.

R.M. (Recoltant-Manipulant): A "grower/producer" who vinifies, bottles, and markets Champagne from grapes he grows. These are the small-production, hand-crafted Champagnes that really define the category. They are worth seeking out.

Quality: Superb to very good.

N.M.s and M.A.s account for 97.3 percent of all Champagne exported. The fact is, most of the really well-made, affordable Champagnes are, by and large, obscure to the average consumer. But please do try to find them. Ask around. Check out a wineshop

with brisk Champagne turnover and more than ten or fifteen labels. Ask several employees to name the best three under-$35 Champagnes in the store. If one of them narrows his eyes and becomes extremely animated, you may have hit pay dirt. If he rattles off the first three big name brands he can think of, move on to plan B. On your own, try to find an R.M. Champagne. Failing that, shop elsewhere.

THE TEST

An excellent way to evaluate the quality of your Champagne is to open it alongside another brand. The best way, of course, is to open it alongside several brands. Make sure at least one of them is R.M.

GETTING THE DAMN THING OPEN

First, forget what you've seen in the movies, locker rooms, and the Indy 500. Champagne is not supposed to be opened with a loud bang and a gushing geyser. At a cost of a dollar or two an ounce, this way madness lies. Rapid carbon dioxide release depletes nearly half of the wine's effervescence. The best approach to opening Champagne should be like life's other great pleasures: Do it slowly.

Take a long, deep breath and remember: *Don't be tense!* You are not preparing to pull the pin out of a live hand grenade. As long as the bottle has not warmed up or been banged about, there is little chance of an embarrassing premature detonation.

Remove and discard the foil and wire cage while keeping the thumb of your other hand on the top of the cork, just in case. During this opening procedure, be sure to angle the bottle away from everyone but detested enemies, as the 6 atmospheres of pressure within can transform the cork into a formidable projectile. Six atmospheres is the equivalent of 90 pounds of pressure per square inch, or that of a fully inflated bus tire. An uncontrolled Champagne cork can explode from the bottle at 40 miles per hour—fast enough to total a Volvo.

Taking the bottle in your left hand, wrap your right hand around the neck, with your thumb and forefinger around the sides of the cork (as though you were holding a quarter on edge), the balance of the right hand grasping the neck below. Now slowly twist, keeping a firm grip on the cork and the neck. Once the cork has been loosened, you should be in total control. *Don't panic!*

Using the mildest of reverse pressure, you should be able to control the cork's slow, easy removal almost to the end, at which point you should smoothly tilt the cork on its side a bit as it leaves the bottle. By turning the cork this way, you will facilitate the softest possible release of gas, and that's crucial. Those precious bubbles now remain captured in the wine rather than hitting the ceiling or hosing down your guests.

This process should be performed entirely under a cloth napkin for two reasons. First, if there is overflow, the napkin will contain it. Second, when you whip the napkin and the cork off the bottle with a bit of flourish at the precise moment of release, you will appear to have magically conjured a wisp of smoke from the opening. Pure showbiz!

Immediately hold the bottle at a 45-degree angle for a few seconds to allow enough air into the neck to prevent any foaming over. This small angling maneuver is extremely effective in completing the "clean opening" of Champagne.

SERVING

The indentation at the bottom of the bottle is known as the *punt,* and although this may seem a precarious maneuver (it is not), place your thumb inside the punt and the palm of your hand up against the underside of the bottle. This is absolutely the most elegant method for serving Champagne, or for that matter any wine whose bottle base contains a punt. This method of pouring is much more secure than it sounds. Practice with a punted bottle filled with water.

Naturally, when pouring this way, the label should always face up proudly; never cover any wine bottle with a napkin while serving. If the bottle is wet from an ice bucket, simply pat it dry with a towel and continue barehanded. Generally, when wines are served

wrapped in a napkin, it is not to emulate "French service"; rather, it is an attempt to camouflage a lousy wine.

STEMWARE

Genuine Champagne, one of mankind's great triumphs, should be treated with an appropriate degree of respect. Champagne glasses should never be served wet or chilled, as this effectively diminishes the Champagne's mousse; it's like pouring beer into a wet glass in order to lessen the head. Always use tall fluted glasses, which show off the glory of Champagne and maintain it. Needless to say, the saucer-shaped glass, said to have been molded from one of Marie Antoinette's breasts, is only good for margaritas, fruit cocktail, and Doris Day movies. The nearly flat surface eradicates Champagne's bubbles in seconds.

TEMPERATURE

As with still white wines, the greater the quality (the complexity of flavor and bouquet), the less chilled a Champagne should be served. Don't diminish a great Champagne by mummifying it in an ice bucket.

BIG IS BETTER

The magnum (two regular bottles) is *the* civilized size for Champagne. Wines tend to mature more gracefully in larger containers, and Champagne even more so. And let's face it, if there are more than two of you, you'll need another bottle anyway (there are only four glasses in a bottle). You should know that half-bottles and splits, which tend to oxidize before they even leave France, are strictly for tourists and the palate-dead.

Practically Useless Wine Knowledge

Those Big Bottles

Magnum — Jeroboam — Rehoboam — Methuselah — Salamanazar — Balthazar — Nebuchadnezzar

WHEN

In a perfect world, everyone would have a glass of Champagne every evening, no later than 6:00 P.M. People with personality problems would begin each day with a glass.

It is the epitome of civility in a clearing in the woods at dusk. It's oh-so-Gershwin on the Brooklyn Bridge. And in a candlelit tub . . .

WINES FOR FOOD

In the history of great cuisine, the peasants were always irrelevant. Only the upper classes got to gorge themselves on caviar and truffles. So it was with the nobility of eighteenth-century France. *Service à la Française,* which could make today's Thanksgiving feast look like a midday snack, consisted of four soups, four fish dishes, four *grands pièces de résistance* roasts, thirty-six side dishes, and a dozen desserts, all served at once. *Mon Dieu!*

After the Revolution, however, the great French chefs saw their customer base shrink precipitously, forcing them to look for work elsewhere in Europe. After all, this type of entertaining requires serious discretionary income. And anyway, nobles without heads can't eat much.

Most of the fleeing French chefs landed in England, where a still-intact, well-heeled upper class could avail themselves of their culinary ministrations. Throughout the nineteenth century, fine dining in England remained a heavy affair. Dinners lasted five hours. Women fainted. Tables groaned under the same heavy French-inspired menus, only now served *à la Russe*—that is, in an organized fashion, appetizer through dessert. As in France of the eighteenth century, the great bawdy reds of Bordeaux, Burgundy, and the Rhône were still considered this cuisine's natural partners.

As the world entered the twentieth century, a fellow named Escoffier codified this cuisine for the first time in writing, so that chefs everywhere could copy the French model. His efforts quickly spread French food throughout Europe; and her wines, sired alongside this opulent fare, became the gold standard. French food and wine easily leaped the Big Pond with our American boys returning home from the First and Second World Wars. By the 1950s and 1960s, French haute cuisine was the undisputed ideal of fine dining in America. The wines, of course, never changed—rich, zaftig French Bordeaux and Burgundy.

Cut to the 1970s. Brave young chefs accept a mission: to explore strange new tastes, to seek out lighter, more healthful foods, to boldly go where no chefs have gone before—nouvelle cuisine! California became a culinary hothouse in the 1970s, her chefs blithely abandoning butter and beef in favor of olive oil and stir-fry. The nouvelle of the seventies opened the door to the global cuisine of the eighties—Japanese, regional Italian, Indonesian, Pacific Rim, Mediterranean, et al. In the nineties we've seen them all fuse and splinter into whimsical combinations of limitless variety. Yet the wines we continue to throw at these vibrant, modern cuisines are the same vinous dinosaurs our parents choked down with Beef Wellington during the Eisenhower administration. The only difference is, today's wines are oakier.

As consumers break out of the stodgy world of "classic" cuisine, free to roam the globe in search of exotic foods without ever having to leave town, the old wine choices no longer apply. It stands to reason that if our foods are now lighter and more dynamic, our wines should be also.

THE STRATEGY

"Okay, smart guy," you're asking now, "so what am I drinking?"

I was afraid you'd ask me that. It's true, the sheer number of the world's foods, and their possible preparations, is daunting. No one could be expected to find a different, individual wine for every dish imaginable, so I won't try. My aim is merely to improve your success rate. To that end, in the pages that follow, I have attempted to break down the world's cuisines into their most basic characteristics, so that suitable wine choices become easy—even fun.

The trick is to identify what the most pronounced flavor and textural elements are in a dish, and target a wine specifically to these elements. Since you now know all about the qualities of the important grape varieties, you should feel confident in choosing a wine that possesses the appropriate: (1) mouthfeel (acidity, alcohol, and tannin), (2) flavor (herbal, earthy, etc.), and (3) sweetness (a little or a lot).

Fortunately, there is a small, highly versatile group of red and white wine grapes that possess higher natural acidity, lower alcohol, and a wider range of styles than their peers. These qualities grant them a very low failure rate with most foods. I call these grapes the "food-friendly seven," and you've certainly met them already in this book. They are Riesling, Chenin Blanc, and Sauvignon Blanc in whites, and Cabernet Franc, Barbera, Gamay, and Pinot Noir in reds. The fact that they are frequently suggested in the following pages simply reflects their inordinately successful applications. Beyond these grapes, though, lie a host of other fascinating wines that make fine, useful alternatives, and in many cases, singularly perfect ones. I will highlight these also as we go.

Please note that I've concentrated on broad categories of foods, without delving into the complexities and subtle flavor combinations found in mythical meals at legendary restaurants. Even in those cases, the principles learned here will serve as well, though you may be tempted to raise the stakes a bit with a more nuanced, hence more expensive, wine. Above all, these choices reflect my own experience with wine and food, and include many of my favorite pairings; but the wine/food combinations below are by no means a rigid curriculum of what works and what doesn't, nor are they meant to be absolute. Experiment.

A FEW HELPFUL DO'S AND DON'TS

Apart from anybody's personal preferences, there are certain chemical reactions that occur when wine and food meet that you should be aware of. There are, in other words, certain constants in the wine/food universe. Before you launch yourself into the cosmos, here they are:

◆ White wine tastes sweeter with artichokes and asparagus. Thus, bone-dry, herbal Sauvignon Blanc works best with them.

◆ White wine tastes metallic with the dark, gray, oily parts of steakfish (bluefish, salmon, tuna).

◆ Red wine tastes metallic with vinegar (salad dressing), shellfish, and snails.

◆ Red wine tannins are softened by dishes with cracked black pepper or fat. Pepper also fleshes out and improves young, fruity reds.

◆ Red meat needs red wines with tannic grip. Tannin behaves like acidity to cleanse the palate.

◆ Salty foods need wines with sweetness, which counteracts salt to achieve balance in the mouth.

◆ Spicy foods need lightweight, low-alcohol, sweet wines. Alcohol fans the flames; sugar douses them.

◆ High-acid foods (those that include citrus or tomato) need high-acid wines. Wines with low acid get flaccid near acid. Ba-dum!

◆ Subtly-flavored foods need more subtle, older wines that have lost their youthful exuberance, like mature Riesling or Bordeaux.

◆ Champagne goes poorly with caviar and smoked salmon. That's right, kids. The sugar dosage in most Champagne is amplified by the pungent fish oils in these foods, turning the wine sweet and fishy. Very dry (older bruts or nondosage) Champagnes can be successful, although icy vodka works best.

◆ Champagne does go well with fried and salty foods, salty nuts and cheeses (Parmigiano), egg dishes (especially with ham or bacon), soups, salads, sushi, and sashimi.

APPETIZERS

There's no point searching for a single wine choice to match the many flavors and textures of any typical assortment of appetizers. All you need is a wine that features racy acidity to stimulate the gastric juices or "work up an appetite." Light appetizers or canapés (literally, "little couches," bread topped with spreads, like cheeses, pâté, etc.) are matched beautifully with crisp, light, dry white wines like **Muscadet** from the Loire and light Italian and Germanic whites. Also **Champagne** and dry sparkling wines made from **Prosecco, Chenin** or **Pinot Blanc.**

Most things we eat before dinner, though, are actually *not* light and frilly. Think about a typical antipasto: a selection of olives, salami, prosciutto, and cheeses. What do they all have in common? *Salt!* The flavor of salty foods is enhanced and balanced best by bright, fruity wines that engage the appetite without filling you up. For whites try **Chenin Blanc,** off-dry **Riesling,** and chilled dry sherries like light **Fino** and tangy **Manzanilla.** For reds, **Beaujolais (Gamay),** light **Pinot Noir,** Loire **Cabernet Franc** wines **(Saumur-Champigny),** and fruity Spanish reds from Navarra.

TIPS

◆ Dramatic or complex wines should be saved for later on in the meal. Their subtleties are squandered on typically straightforward appetizer selections.

- Typical bourgeois American starters—like cheeses, chips, dips, and pigs-in-blankets—lean to the salty side, to put it mildly. Stick with juicy, fruity Germanic whites or **Manzanilla sherry** as a foil to the salt and grease of these appetizers.

- Fried appetizers really rock with sparkling wines. The textural interplay between the oily mouthfeel of fried food and the cleansing sensation of tiny bubbles is a real turn-on.

- Tapas—the traditional Spanish bar food that started out as finger-sized portions and evolved to the size of American appetizers—are rich, oily, and salty. From Spain, try **Cava** (sparkling wine), crisp, citrusy **Albarino** (Spain's greatest white), or salty **Manzanilla sherry** served up cold in little *copitas* (sherry glasses).

SALADS AND VEGETABLES

Whether it's salad served with a citrus- or vinegar-based dressing, or vegetables in any style, both cry out for a green, herbaceous wine with razor-sharp acidity to counteract their mouth-tingling qualities.

Beyond **Beaujolais** and other light, tart **Gamay** wines, this is purely white wine territory. Try fresh, zippy **Ugni Blanc (Trebbiano** from Gascogne), German **Rieslings** of trocken (very dry) level, nonoaked New Zealand **Sauvignon Blanc**, nonvintage **Champagne,** or other dry sparklers.

SEAFOOD

Like the wedge of lemon at the side of the plate, acidity in wine acts as a juicy foil for fish. That lemon ain't just garnish—it brightens and defines the flavor of seafood while cutting funky fish oils. Ditto for the wine.

Shellfish: Raw, Steamed, and Broiled

Nowhere are high acid and light body more important in a wine than when it's served with shellfish. Light whites are essential here. They make a perfect counterpoint to the richness and brininess of shellfish. In fact, the concept of light, delicate white wines being amplified and fleshed out by richer foods is nowhere more perfectly realized than in the arena of shellfish.

A good place to start might be with **Sauvignon Blanc** (nonoaked!). Look for **Sancerre, Pouilly-Fumé,** and **Ménétou-Salon** from the Loire, as well as Sauvignons from New Zealand and South Africa. Other interesting choices include bright, citrusy **Albarino** from Rias Baixas in Spain and Burgundy's unloved, nervy **Aligoté** (the classic base wine for kir). Fresh, new **Muscadet** is a wonderful light, crisp, under-$10 choice, as is green, spritzy **Vinho Verde** from Portugal (especially in summer). To coax out the savvy, adventurous foodie in you, try **Vouvray** sec (**Chenin Blanc** at its dry, flashy best) or flinty **Sylvaner** from Germany's Rheinhessen. Trocken (bone dry) or halbtrocken (half-dry) German **Rieslings** are a brilliant choice with shellfish, of course. The rich weight and pungent green aroma of premier cru or grand cru **Chablis** make a classic pairing with sweeter shellfish like lobster and king crab.

If you find yourself in a restaurant thinking about raw clams or oysters, and things are looking pretty pathetic in the nonoaked white wine department, scan the wine list for any non-Champagne sparkling wine or those made with Pinot Noir and Chardonnay. Try **Prosecco** or other light Italian sparklers, Spanish **Cava,** or German **Sekt.** High acidity is the critical component here, but without the strong varietal signature of Pinot Noir and Chardonnay. In other words, don't waste your dough on a good Champagne here (not that you have any possible chance of finding a good Champagne on most wine lists); the dish would wreck it anyway, as it would the dish.

Avoid American Sauvignon Blanc (Fumé Blanc). California's warm climate creates overly aggressive herbal flavors and weak acidity, all compounded by the addition of oak, which turns the flavor of shellfish thin and metallic.

Shellfish: Sautéed and Fried

The addition of butter or oil adds an unctuous, oily mouthfeel to the equation; hence you'll need to turn up the weight of the wine, and certainly its ripeness. Try off-dry, demi-sec **Vouvray** or Kabinett- or Spätlese-grade **Rieslings.** Also, sparklers like **Crémant d'Alsace** (Pinot Blanc), sparkling **Vouvray** (Chenin Blanc), or German **Sekt**—usually made from Riesling or Pinot Blanc. If you find a retailer with good, fresh sparkling Vouvray or Sekt, send him a dozen roses each year on his birthday—you have a real friend.

Mild/Delicate Fish—Sautéed, Poached

Sole, fluke, flounder, trout, freshwater bass or sea bass, halibut, ocean sturgeon, catfish, and orange roughy. Delicate fish in rich, elegant sauces show off finer, more delicate wines. Choosing wines for this category presents the classic conundrum: In the desire to serve as fine a wine as possible with any cuisine, the diner feels that a more expensive wine should be a better wine. While this may be true by and large, the theory quickly reaches a point of diminishing return. The overwhelming majority of the world's more expensive (over $20) wines are rich and opulent, and simply inappropriate for mild, delicate fish. Buck up. The best wines for this food are inexpensive. Elegant **Sancerres** and **Pouilly-Fumés**, a wide variety of Italian whites (rarely over $10 or $15), **Muscadet**, **Chablis**, and Mosel **Rieslings** are all superior choices.

Fatty/Oily Fish—Sautéed, Fried, Grilled

Salmon, tuna, swordfish, lake sturgeon, mackerel, pompano, sardines, anchovies, and bluefish. More important than cooking method in marrying these dishes with wine are the fattiness and strong individual flavors of the fish themselves. These swimmers require lots of everything—acid, body, and flavor. That means big whites and light reds.

WHITE

Heady Alsace **Tokay Pinot Gris, Riesling**, and **Gewürztraminer**, and those outrageous Spätlese and even Auslese-weight Brunnhildes from the Mosel and the Rhine are among the best, or large-scale **Chenin Blanc** wines from the Loire, like demi-sec **Vouvray** and **Savennières**. You can even wheel out some of those 90-point white wines that are rapidly deteriorating in your cellar:

wild, over-the-top white **Burgundies** (Chardonnay) like **Meursault, Puligny, Corton-Charlemagne,** and the **Montrachets;** or any of those crazy, exotic, pear-scented Rhône varietals like **Viognier, Marsanne,** and **Roussanne.** These grapes account for wines like **Hermitage Blanc, Châteauneuf du Pape blanc,** and **Condrieu** ($25 to $50). I find that these extravagant wines, like most southern whites, lack the real acid cut that's a must for most foods, but if there is a place at the table for these flavorful oddities, it's with sautéed fish. Make sure they're young.

RED

Light **Pinot Noirs** from California and Oregon, **Sancerre Rouge** from the Loire, and only the lightest of red **Burgundies** are fine. But my hands-down choice of red wine for fish is herb-scented Loire **Cabernet Franc,** including **Saumur-Champigny, Chinon,** and **Bourgueil.** Don't forget, there's invariably something green or herbal on a fish plate. Only Cabernet Franc among reds is herbal when well made. **Beaujolais** (Gamay) and **Barbera** are also suitable, especially for heavily grilled (caramelized) steakfish.

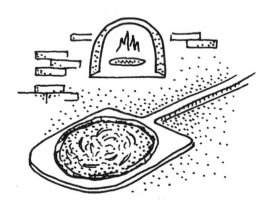

PIZZA

Italy's greatest fast food (the heavier American version notwithstanding) contains two distinctive wine-challenging ingredients: tomato sauce and cheese. In order to match the pronounced acidity of tomato sauce, the first element in your wine choice must be high acid. The second element must marry with the saltiness of cheese. This is accomplished with ripe, sweet fruit.

No mystery here: a light, fruity, high-acid red. For Italian purists, **Barbera, Dolcetto,** and young, inexpensive **Chianti.** For sinners, lighter-styled **Zinfandels** (red, of course), **Pinot** and **Petite Syrah** from California, and Australian **Shiraz.**

Sausage or pepperoni with that pie? Bring in those big, dark southern Italian reds like **Salice Salentino** and **Primitivo** from Apulia. Add peppers? Herbal **Cabernet Franc** is a must.

PASTA

Pasta's what you put on it. It's the handiest culinary vehicle, carrying everything from simple tomato sauce with fresh basil to something rich and brown, laced with strips of wild boar. Pasta can reflect any cook's most personal palate. I myself, being a cement-headed indigenist, prefer my pasta with Italian wines, and the possibilities are nearly limitless. There's an old wine wheeze about Italy's being one giant vineyard. It's true, of course, but as with the world's other great wine regions, some grape varieties consistently perform better with food than others.

Red Sauce

Only lemons and limes have higher acidity than tomatoes. You'll need a high-acid red wine with a touch of sweetness to balance a red sauce's acidity and to match its fruit flavor. My two favorite workaday Italian red grapes for food are **Barbera**, the undisputed king of Italian high-acid reds, and herbal **Cabernet Franc**. Cabernet Franc, a northern-grown red wine grape, is sometimes labeled varietally, but it is also a primary component of **Franciacorta Rosso**, where it displays the same wonderful herbal note and bell pepper aroma as it does in the Loire Valley's **Chinon** and **Bourgueil**.

Red Sauce With . . .

When you enrich the classic red sauce, either with veal or with wild mushrooms and vegetables, **Barbera** and **Cabernet Franc** wines can be joined by fleshy, medium-bodied reds like **Montepulciano** in its many incarnations, from **Montepulciano d'Abruzzo** to

Rosso Cònero; fruitier versions of **Sangiovese**, like light **Chianti** or **Morellino**; and sappy **Dolcetto** from Piedmont.

Add bacon, sautéed onions, sausages, or gamy meats to your red sauce, and you'll need to crank up the sweetness in your wine. Go south for value. That's where heady, sultry reds are born. The sun-baked regions of Puglia, Calabria, and Basilicata (the toe, the heel, and the laces of the Italian boot) offer manly grapes like **Negroamaro** ("black and bitter"), **Primitivo** (antecedent of American **Zinfandel**), and **Aglianico** (ancient Campanian grape of the Caesars). The requisite sweetness and body can also be achieved with oak-aged *(barrique)* **Barbera**.

Primavera and Light Cream Sauces

Pasta primavera, vegetable lasagnas, and other vegetable and light cream sauces call for light, refreshing, and generally less expensive white wines like **Soave** and **Bianco di Custoza** (Veneto), **Orvieto** (Umbria), or **Pinot Grigio** (lots of places), and light, fruity, under-$10 reds like lighter **Valpolicellas** (Veneto), **Montepulcianos** (Abruzzi), light-style **Chiantis** (Toscana), and nonoaked **Barberas**. My personal hands-down favorite, however, is sparkling **Prosecco** from the Veneto.

Heavy Cream Sauces

Alfredo, gorgonzola, carbonara, and other thick, rich, cheesy sauces require light- to medium-bodied wines with heightened acidity to cut through the dish's creamy mouthfeel. If this description sounds like white wine, you're correct. The way these rich, creamy dishes amplify a wine's body and alcohol makes red wines seem bloated and hot. Try crisp **Pinot Bianco** or **Sauvignon Blanc** from Alto Adige or Collio.

Pesto

The classic match for pesto—the oily, basil-based sauce from Genoa—is nonoaked **Sauvignon Blanc** (herbal with herbal) or stony **Gavi (Cortese)** from Piedmont, Genoa's inseparable northern neighbor. My interest has been piqued in recent years by a fascinating, anise-scented grape called **Arneis** from Piedmont. Arneis ($15 to $20 for good examples) is a weird and wondrous white varietal anomaly in a predominantly red wine region. Though somewhat lower in acidity than one might hope, its distinctive, opulently herbal aroma provides it easy access to this difficult-to-match uncooked sauce.

Shellfish

Clams, mussels, scungilli, calamari, shrimp, crab, and lobster need crisp, light- to medium-weight, low-to-average alcohol (10 to 12%) white wines to counterbalance their richness. Italian whites are tailor-made for pasta with shellfish, and the choices abound. Two excellent choices are flinty, mineral-redolent **Gavi** from Piedmont, and **Verdicchio,** the anise-scented white grape of the Marches on the Adriatic coast. What I particularly crave with pasta and shellfish, however, is the quintessential Italian aperitivo—light, frothy, citrus-scented **Prosecco** from the Veneto. Sparkling Prosecco deserves to be better known. It is a versatile, food-friendly white wine that just happens to possess the textural bonus of bubbles. At about $11 a bottle, fresh, well-made Prosecco can easily substitute nearly anytime a light, dry white is called for. Prosecco . . . the foodie's friend.

Most red wine/shellfish combinations cause an iodine-tainted disaster in your mouth. Be warned.

ROASTED MEATS

Slow roasting creates complexity in meats as well as succulent texture and the sort of natural juiciness that is usually found only in wine. The absence of grill marks, charcoal, or spicy sauces that can mask the pure essence of meat flavors allows complex, mature wines to strut their stuff without competing with a lot of distractions.

When most people see that beef is on the menu, they head for the biggest, boldest reds. Yet, with few exceptions, beef does not offer that strong a flavor. Lamb, game, even duck have much more reason to be accompanied by big inky brutes. Unless a barbecue sauce or serious glaze is involved, stick with the more elegant or mature reds.

That said, there are more vinous possibilities with roasted meats than with any other food group. It's a golden opportunity to show off your best Sunday red. Amen.

GAME

Duck, goose, partridge, squab, quail, grouse, ostrich, venison, boar, elk, moose, caribou, and other horny game

Pungent, chewy, full-blooded dark meats and birds with both brown and sweet fruit sauces need wines that are their equal—strapping, sappy reds. Near-black wines that coat the palate and stain the teeth. Red **Burgundies** and other large-scaled **Pinots** can work exceptionally well with game birds, while young, broad-shouldered **Bordeaux** (Médoc and St.-Estèphe) and ruddy **Hermitage (Syrah)** from the Rhône stand up smartly alongside footed game. From France's sprawling southwest, **Cahors (Malbec)** and **Madiran (Tannat)** are also terrific choices and from Italy, earthy **Barolos (Nebbiolo)** and rich, leathery **Brunellos (Sangiovese)**.

When sweet fruits and sauces are added, or heavy caramelization by grilling and glazing occurs, you'll want to lose some of these less ripe wines. The wines that marry *most* beautifully with these sweeter styles of game preparations have not only the grit and extract but also the requisite sweetness to match. Sappy, bacon-scented **Côte Rôtie** from the northern Rhône, deep, jammy Australian **Shiraz (Syrah)**, and big, brambly American **Zinfandel** make sublime game mates. With sweeter game bird preparations, pungent, velvety, late-harvest **Amarone** from the Veneto can fashion one of the planet's sexiest wine–food marriages.

To tenderize a tough cut of game, marinate with some of the same wine you plan to serve and join the two at the table. Voilà!

PICNICS

Typical picnic foods invariably include vegetables, greens, and pasta salads (mayonnaise or vinaigrette dressings), cold meats and poultry, cheeses and fruits.

Drink light, fruity reds made from the food-friendly grapes: **Cabernet Franc, Barbera, Pinot Noir,** and **Gamay.** Also, lighter red **Zinfandels,** sappy **Valpolicella** from the Italian Veneto, and all manner of rosés. You want to look for wines that have high acidity and fruitiness and are low enough in alcohol to be served cool—what we call chillable reds. When in doubt, there's no more chillable, high-acid, fruity red than fresh, young **Beaujolais (Gamay).**

Ethnic Cuisines

ITALY

Italy has a culinary history as rich and storied as that of France—or anywhere else—and her cuisine is just as subtle and complex. Perhaps more than in any other country, though, wine and food in Italy form a magnificent natural synergy. They just taste great together.

As I have with France, I have divided Italy into three culinary regions, based on the shared general character of foods and wines in each. Nonregional matches are noted.

Northern

The foods of Piedmont and its environs are most influenced by the cuisine of its closest neighbors—France, Switzerland, and the convoluted mélange that was once Yugoslavia. It is rich but subtle. Ingredients focus on potatoes, rice (risotto), polenta, mushrooms, truffles, cheese, and veal, beef, lamb, and game. Butter is the cooking medium, and very little garlic is used. Wines for this food vary widely.

As a source for mouthwatering, food-friendly whites, northern Italy is where the action is. **Pinot Grigio, Pinot Bianco** and **Soave,** as well as crisp, stony **Gavi** from Piedmont, beautifully suit the North's regional fish and shellfish. Sparkling **Prosecco** from the Veneto is a blissful accompaniment to most seafood—especially fried seafood. For seafood risotto, try **Tocai** from Friuli.

For veal, beef, and mushroom risottos, **Franciacorta Rosso (Cabernet Franc, Barbera,** and **Merlot),** or aged **Nebbiolo** wines, like **Barolo, Barbaresco** and **Spanna.**

For lamb and game dishes, turn up the weight and sweetness with big, unctuous reds like younger **Nebbiolo** (good grip for fatty meats), barrique **Barbera** (great acidity combined with nice sweetness), and thick, sweet, sensual **Amarone (Corvina, Molinara,** and **Rondinella**—hey, that sounds like a law firm).

Central

Tuscan cuisine combines the olive oil based cooking of Tuscany with the butter-and-cream-sauced cuisine of Emilio Romagna. Filled pastas, grilled meats and vegetables, bean soups with pasta, prosciutto, and balsamic vinegar are the fixings.

The best white wines for vegetables, seafood, and light pastas are crisp **Orvieto (Trebbiano** and **Garganega)** from Umbria, nutty Tuscan **Vernaccia di San Gimignano,** and anise-scented **Verdicchio** from the Marches on the Adriatic coast.

For salty hams and cheeses and meat-filled pastas, you need fruity **Sangiovese** reds like **Morellino** and **Rosso di Montalcino.**

With grilled meats you can present your best Classico and Riserva **Chiantis, Vino Nobile di Montepulciano,** and **Brunello di Montalcino,** all made from the noble **Sangiovese.**

Nonregional matches: For salty hams and cheeses, fruity northern reds like **Valpolicella (Corvina, Molinara,** and **Rondinella), Barbera,** and **Dolcetto** would be among my first choices.

For sautéed rabbit with olive oil and fresh rosemary, light **Chiantis** from Colli Senesi or **Rufina** are classic partners.

Sicily and the South

It's hot, it's poor, and the women are veddy beeyootiful. This is great, lusty food, teeming with olive oil, tomatoes, garlic, salty fish, and sheep cheeses; also, fruits and nuts as seasonings, and pasta, lamb, and sausages all over the place. The red wines from this part of Italy are roasted, sweet, and earthy—perfect indigenous choices.

Greco and **Fiano** from Campania and **Vermentino** from Sardinia are the local white wine high points.

Red wines include a host of choices from grapes like **Aglianico, Primitivo, Negroamaro,** and **Galioppo,** all with suitable machismo for the rich, piquant dishes of southern Italy and her islands.

GERMANY, AUSTRIA, AND THE SCANDINAVIAN COUNTRIES

If ever there was a cuisine that needed high-acid wines, it has to be here in the clogged aorta of modern Europe, bunker of bland, carbo-driven, fat-loaded meat-and-potato dishes.

MEAT: Pork, veal, venison, goose, and lots of sausages

FISH: Cured, pickled, grilled, and smoked

VEGETABLES: Cabbage, including sauerkraut, and all manner of roots, like beets, potatoes, and turnips

GRAIN: Dumplings (spaetzle) and black breads

SEASONINGS: A few herbs and spices—caraway seed, allspice, paprika, juniper, and dill head the short list; garlic, onions, and leeks.

DAIRY: A variety of cow's-milk cheeses, running the gamut from mild Emmenthaler to nutty Gruyère to room-clearing Limburger.

WINES: **Germanics, Germanics, Germanics** (see Germanics, page 68) and any of the food-friendly reds: **Cabernet Franc, Barbera, Gamay** and **Pinot Noir.**

◆ Though it is said that in the past decade Germanic cuisine has been reinventing itself in a more modern, health-conscious manner, the world at large has yet to experience the outcome.

◆ The overall flavor palette of this cuisine is . . . beige.

FRANCE

Everyone loves to disparage the French, and I'm no exception. But you can't argue with success—namely, the world's greatest food and *six* of the food-friendly seven grapes! Riesling, Chenin Blanc, Sauvignon Blanc, Cabernet Franc, Gamay, and Pinot Noir *all* flourish here. Only Italy's Barbera is absent.

What to drink with the fabulous foods of France? Like Italy, France has such a wealth of high-quality native wines and wine-food traditions that I will confine my recommendations to her wines exclusively. I have divided France into three culinary regions, each with its own indigenous wine-food subculture. On the occasions when nonregional matches make sense, I have noted them as well.

Northern and Central

This is the home of haute cuisine, where it's the sauce that counts. Subtle yet complex butter-and-cream-based sauces, fines herbes (tarragon, chives, parsley, chervil), eggs, Dijon mustard, and heavily reduced stocks are the dynamic elements of this food. Bold, rich, high-acid wines are de rigueur here.

For salads, escargot, oysters, light vegetable and fish dishes, or anything that swims in a light cream sauce, serve **Champagne** (only nondosage with oysters), Loire **Sauvignons (Sancerre, Pouilly-Fumé,** etc.), and Loire **Chenins (Vouvray** and **Montlouis).**

For fattier fish and thicker sauces, go for big dry whites: **Savennières (Chenin Blanc)** from the Loire and heady **Chardonnay** wines from Chablis and Burgundy.

For lighter meats like veal, pork, and white meat birds, serve the juicy **Gamay** wines of Beaujolais and herb-scented **Cabernet Francs** from the Loire (**Saumur, Chinon, Bourgueil,** etc.).

For red meat and game birds, **Bordeaux** and red **Burgundies** are no-brainers, no matter what the sauce.

Nonregional matches: For fattier fish and lighter meats, I'd choose Alsace whites over white Burgundies every time.

Provence and the Southwest

This region, a sort of giant herb garden, is powerfully driven by Mediterranean influences. As such, its ingredients have much in common with other Mediterranean cuisines—Italy and Spain in particular. Seafood and game are prepared with vivid seasoning—anchovies, dried herbs, fennel/anise, eggplant, peppers, zucchini, olives, prunes, tomato-based sauces, and plenty of olive oil. In the far west of the region, cholesterol runs amok, with rich foie gras and Southwest France's seminal gustatory triumph—pork and duck cassoulet. Peasant food for well-fed peasants.

For seafood, high-acid native whites are hard to find, though razor-sharp **Ugni Blanc** from Gascogne and a plethora of local rosés serve well enough.

For rich seafood and lighter meats try heavily perfumed whites from **Viognier, Roussanne,** and **Marsanne,** like **Côtes-du-Rhône Blanc** up through **Condrieu** and **Hermitage Blanc.**

For all that pâté, goose liver, duck, and boar, you have my permission to go as insane as you like with inky over-the-top red wines. Black wines like **Cahors (Malbec),** fierce **Madiran (Tannat),** and dusty **Bandol (Mourvèdre)** are up to the task. Also, pungent, peppery **Syrah-Grenache** blends from Châteauneuf du Pape and Gigondas, Côtes de Roussillon, Côtes de Lubéron, Corbières,

St.-Chinian, and Minervois. And, of course, the great **Syrah** triumphs of the northern Rhône, **Cornas**, **Côte-Rôtie**, and **Hermitage.**

Nonregional matches: Rich seafood, light meats, and sausages unmask the South of France's vinous Achilles heel. No high-acid reds in residence. Good **Beaujolais** fits right in here.

Alsace

Alsace has the most Michelin-starred restaurants in France, but essentially Alsatian cuisine is French sauces on German food. Big on cheese, too. Choucroute garni (sausages, pork, ham, goose, and potatoes on a bed of steaming sauerkraut seasoned with juniper berries) pretty much typifies the hearty and savory foods of Alsace. Big, sassy, aromatic white wines are what's called for, and in France, Alsace has the market cornered.

Beginning with **Alsace Pinot Blanc**, one of the world's best $10 white wine bargains, you can wend your way through huge, oily **Rieslings** (the world's heftiest examples of the variety), move on to deep, succulent **Tokay Pinot Gris**, and with luck alight, still standing, astride powerful, rose-petal-and-lychee-scented **Gewürztraminer.** Whew!

SPICY FOODS OF THE WESTERN HEMISPHERE, OR CAN'T I JUST HAVE A BEER WITH THAT?

Yes, a beer goes very nicely with spicy fare. It's got the three balms for spicy food: sweetness (from malt), low alcohol, and bubbles. But if you're so inclined, here's the wine story: Heat in food exaggerates everything in a wine. High-alcohol wines, even those barely over

11%, can feel as fiery as brandy in a mouth reeling from habanero chile peppers. When served with spicy foods, subtle or complex wines are wasted. Tannic reds are a disaster. Oaked wines, red or white, should be absolutely avoided; they are particularly nasty when wedded to spicy foods. So what does that leave for wine fans?

Riesling and **Beaujolais.** God bless 'em.

Here's why. Neither wine is ever oaked or tannic or ever climbs above 11 or 12% alcohol. More important is the sweetness issue. The havoc spicy foods wreak in the mouth leaves only the tip of the tongue capable of flavor recognition—and of course that's where the sweet spot is. Beaujolais is always sweet and fruity, and Riesling can be selected at any degree of sweetness you like.

Tex-Mex/Southwestern

Beef and pork, sweet corn flavors, heated up by jalapeño and poblano chiles. This cuisine asks too much of wines when much heat is present. Red-wine food when it's not too hot. **Beaujolais (Gamay).**

Mexican

Beef, pork, chicken, and seafood. Chile peppers of various heats are the basic Mexican seasoning. By comparison with Tex-Mex, Mexican has more citrus, fresh herbs, tomatoes, and gloppy bean sauces, *and* more refined sauces *(moles)* that are complemented by richer reds like Rhône-style California reds from grapes like **Carignan, Syrah,** and **Mourvèdre.** For whites, riper **Riesling** and other Germanics apply. For reds, **Cabernet Franc** is superb, especially with the more herbal dishes. Other suitable reds include **Beaujolais** and **Barbera d'Asti** and yes, even a fruity sangría. A classic Mexican dish, ceviche (raw fish marinated in lime juice), is best matched with sparkling **Prosecco,** sparkling **Vouvray,** or **Riesling Sekt.** But watch out! When the jalapeños begin to make the top of your head perspire, only the lightest, sweetest wines can quench the flames.

Caribbean

Lamb, goat, dried fish, fried foods, frittered everything from conch to vegetables to plantains; jerk seasoning (smoky barbecue), allspice, and habanero chiles. This is heavy, saucy food. Try sparkling wines for fried dishes (except red meat), **Riesling,** of course, and light, fruity reds. Dishes that are fired up by habanero chiles singe the mouth and represent a fine opportunity to unload any sweet, clumsy California **Johannisberg Riesling** or typically coarse, overdosaged mass-market **Champagne** you may have lying around. A young, fresh **Spanish** Tinto (**Rioja** or **Navarra**) works nicely with the milder meat dishes of this cuisine.

Cajun/Creole

Seafood, shellfish, sausages and other pork products, fried foods, rice dishes, jambalaya and *étouffée* (seafood stew). French herbs like thyme and savory, greens, okra (whose mucilaginous melt-down creates the glue of gumbo), all fired up with cayenne pepper. Beer refreshes the palate best with this kind of food, with **Riesling** and **Beaujolais** a close second.

INDIAN AND ASIAN

Thai and Vietnamese, or Nam Pla Meets Nuoc Mam

It's important to note that Thai and Vietnamese dishes involve all the components of taste sensation: sweet, sour, salty, bitter, and hot. Crisp salads, noodle dishes, and seafood are seasoned with combinations of the following: basil, fresh coriander, coconut milk, curry pastes, piri piri (hot mini–chile peppers), garlic, ginger, soy-based or fish sauce, peanut sauce, and citrus (kaffir lime, lemon-grass). A fresh sense of green herbs also characterizes this cuisine, which should ring a bell as a wine clue. Green and herbal! Try **Sauvignon Blanc** and **Chenin Blanc** for fish and vegetable dishes; and although the sweet/salty flavors in this cuisine more often complement whites than reds (whites seem to soothe, while reds can taste metallic and hot), **Cabernet Franc**'s herb-redolent, sweet, juicy character makes it a safe haven for red lovers.

Indian

This cuisine is definitely not about a single flavor. Typical Indian dishes have as many as fifteen different herbs and spices blended into a single curry powder. Then vegetables, lamb or chicken, bas-mati rice (aromatic), fresh coriander, tropical fruits, yogurt, and high-acid accompaniments (tamarind), hot peppers, and mango chutney (sweet/sour/hot) are tossed in. Also, there seems to be no such thing in Indian cooking as "mildly hot." It's either mild or *very* hot. Wine geeks, give it up! No wine can match Indian food's complexity head to head. Wine should take more of a back seat function as a kind of palate refresher.

Light whites from Italy, low-alcohol German **Riesling** and **Gewürztraminer,** and perhaps demi-sec **Vouvray (Chenin).** After that, light lager beer and pale ale. For reds, you know the drill. **Beaujolais** and **Cabernet Franc.** In fact, I would probably not recommend wine at all with the hotter preparations.

Chinese

In Chinese cuisine, as well as in Thai and Indian, texture is as important as flavor. Every facet of each bite is detailed. Each small flavor and texture, a perfection of silkiness or crunch. The importance of textural considerations in Chinese cooking necessitates texturally exciting wines. In most cases, stick with the food-friendly seven: **Riesling, Chenin Blanc, Sauvignon Blanc, Cabernet Franc, Gamay, Barbera,** and **Pinot Noir.** In fact, Chinese food provides the one culinary arena where *all* of the food-friendly seven can happily gather and frolic.

SZECHUAN AND HUNAN

These are the cuisines of central and western China. Typical dishes involve spicy and hot-and-sour sauces, dried chiles, most meats and many vegetables, noodles, dumplings, soy sauce, sesame oil, ginger, and garlic. By and large, as Americans experience it, this is *spicy* Chinese food. Light-bodied wines with high acidity and significant sweetness are able to refresh the palate and punch their way through this cuisine's heat and pungency. Sweet, low-alcohol Spätlese- and Auslese-level **Rieslings**, as well as demi-sec **Vouvray (Chenin Blanc)** and even light, frothy **Moscato d'Asti**, act as a balm in the blaze of hot chile oil. Only Sauvignon Blanc is inappropriate here—not sweet enough. While all the food-friendly reds are acceptable at the Szechuan/Hunan table, spicier menu selections call for the lighter, lower-alcohol grape varieties. **Gamay (Beaujolais)** and light **Cabernet Franc (Saumur-Champigny)** are best bets.

CANTONESE

Cantonese cuisine casts a wide culinary net: delicate, herb-perfumed steamed fish and shellfish at one end, and lusty barbecued pork and duck at the other. Stylistically, Cantonese is sweeter and less spicy and leans toward grander presentations. Fermented soy beans (called black beans) and sweet-and-sour treatments are typical. All manner of soy-based preparations, from steamed and sautéed fish and vegetables to Americanized dishes like fried rice, egg foo young, and dumplings, are salty; and salty food requires high-acid whites. Amazingly, as long as a wine offers juicy acidity, both very dry and sweetly ripe wines can be enjoyed—even with the very same dish! **Riesling** (Trocken up through Spätlese), **Chenin Blanc** (sec or demi-sec), and crisp, nonoaked **Sauvignon Blancs** drink beautifully with soy-influenced dishes. Red wine choices include, of course, the food-friendly four; but with roasted and barbecued meats, other sweet reds with more body are not only acceptable but necessary. You may wheel out your big chewy fruit bombs, like California **Cabernet** and **Zinfandel**, Australian **Shiraz**, and even **Amarone**, if that's your yen.

Sparkling wine with dumplings or dim sum are a natural together.

The outsized reds listed above, as well as Auslese-level **Rieslings**, commit a hedonistic, sweet coupling with the crackly fat of Peking duck.

If you add more red meats to Szechuan, you kind of get Korean. Choose your wines accordingly.

Japanese

Though **sake**, the traditional Japanese rice wine, makes a soothing, natural partner to much of Japan's cuisine, there are applicable, even exciting, wine possibilities.

SUSHI AND SASHIMI

Perhaps the most elegant and detailed of the world's cuisines, sushi and sashimi are the pure "Zen essence" of fish. Light, high-acid wines with little or no residual sweetness are the only choice. Crisp, bone-dry, neutral **Muscadet** from the Loire and steely, Trocken (very dry) **Riesling** from Germany perform impeccably here, but my favorites are non-Champagne sparklers like **Prosecco** from Italy's Veneto, sparkling **Vouvray** (Loire), and Trocken **Riesling Sekt** (sparkling). I suggest "non-Champagne" sparklers because of the strong varietal impact of Champagne's Chardonnay/Pinot Noir makeup and its added sugar dosage. Dry and light are best here.

TEMPURA AND SUKIYAKI

Tempura—and all other light, fried food—is best accompanied by sparkling wines from Champagne, as well as the non-Champagne sparklers mentioned above. The additional fruitiness of Champagne does not detract from the flavors of deep-fried seafood, vegetables, and light meats. As for broth-based dishes like sukiyaki, still wine has no texture to latch onto. Sparklers are a must, and it's back to non-Champagne types again.

TERIYAKI AND GRILLED MEATS

Salty soy meets sweet mirin! Whether it's seafood, beef, chicken, pork, or a prehistoric dinosaur frozen in the polar ice cap and thawed out by an atomic test gone horribly wrong, only fruity, high-acid wines will save Tokyo. With seafood, chicken, and pork, demi-sec **Vouvray (Chenin Blanc)** or Spätlese **Riesling** is delicious and refreshing. With beef, drink juicy **Beaujolais (Gamay)** or light **Cabernet Franc** wines like **Saumur-Champigny.** An exceptionally magical conjuring with teriyaki-glazed salmon (grilled or broiled) is light California or Oregon **Pinot Noir.**

Cheese

Cheese is a mystery to most people, sort of like North Korea or automobile transmissions. As such, it is the food world's least understood and most undervalued glory. Where wine is concerned, fine cheese, with its unique, creamy mouthfeel and salty, savory character, can transform even a simple workaday wine into a celestial beverage. Cheese is so efficient in this regard that unscrupulous wine merchants often insist that it be served when tasting with customers. This questionable tactic enables them to unload even the harshest, unsalable plonk with relative ease.

Take note, though. The "fine cheese" of which I speak is *not* the typical machine-made, pasteurized, homogenized, lobotomized cheeselike product on your grocery store shelf. This "cheese" is the equivalent of jug wine—serviceable at best. Truly great cheese (only marginally more expensive than the "synthetic" stuff, though slightly trickier to find) is a handmade creation—an artisanal food. Ask for it. Demand it. Shop elsewhere to find it.

Most people assume that red is the only type of wine to serve with cheese. Balderdash, I say! Whites and sparkling wines, with their higher acidity and lower alcohol, are often superior choices for many of the same cheeses with which red wines are successful. Experiment with various combinations.

Here, then, are some classic wine/cheese matchups, as well as a few quirky suggestions of my own. Each group of cheeses below begins with the easier-to-find examples and proceeds to the more obscure "cheese shop" gems.

Cheeses

Rich Double- and Triple-Cream Cheeses

Examples: L'Explorateur, Saint-André, Gratte-Paille, Boursault, Pierre Robert

These 60 to 75% butterfat French cheeses, created by adding extra cream to the fresh curd, need crisp, palate-cleansing wines with serious acidity. Outrageous cheeses require extreme vinous measures. My favorite, **Champagne**, creates a sublime textural foil for these unctuous, hedonistic cheeses. Another way to go is in the opposite direction, rich with rich. Big, sweet, sweet, fortified wines from high-acid white grapes: **Oloroso sherry, Bual Madeira,** or **Hungarian Tokay.**

Other Soft Ripened Cheeses

Examples: Brie, Camembert, Italian Toma

These cheeses go nicely with sparkling wines, but you may also consider fresh, lively reds like **Beaujolais, Saumur-Champigny (Cabernet Franc** from the Loire), **Pinot Noir** from California or Burgundy, or light **Bordeaux.**

Full-Flavored, Semisoft Cheeses

Examples: Gouda, Emmental, St. Nectaire, Fontina d'Aosta, Morbier, Tomme de Savoie

These cheeses have a rich creaminess that melds well with white wines. The fuller, more complex flavors of these cheeses, though, require wines with strong character. Bring on those big white Burgundies like **Meursault (Chardonnay), Alsatian Riesling,** or **Tokay Pinot Gris,** and luscious demi-sec **Vouvray (Chenin Blanc)** from the Loire.

Semi-hard Cheeses

Examples: Cheddar, Cheshire, Gruyère, Greek Kasseri, Comte, Spanish Mahon

Now we're talking about deep, rich, complex flavors coming from both wine and cheese. For the Cheddar, Greek, and Spanish cheeses, choose rich yet soft reds like **Montepulciano d'Abruzzo,**

Rioja, and **Bordeaux**-style (**Cabernet**-based) reds. The nutty cheeses in this category, like Comte and Gruyère, actually marry up best with Alpine whites such as **Tokay d'Alsace** and Austrian **Gruner Veltliner.** Smoked examples of these cheeses, which are saltier and oilier, are beautifully accompanied by fruitier Germanic whites: **Riesling, Scheurebe,** and **Gewürztraminer.**

Goat Cheese (Chèvre)

Examples: Montrachet, Caprini, Boucheron, Crottin de Chavignol, French Valençay, Catalan Garrotxa, Chabichou du Poitou

Zesty, herbal goat cheese needs a juicy, herbal white wine, and that means **Sauvignon Blanc.** It really is that simple. The traditional source, and still one of the best for **Sauvignon,** is the Loire valley in northwest France. **Sancerre, Pouilly-Fumé,** and **Ménétou-Salon** all make lovely, light partners for chèvre. Better Sauvignons ($15 to $20) from South Africa are an interesting alternative, but brassy, olive-scented Sauvignon wines from New Zealand have the additional body necessary for more aggressive, herb-covered chèvres. Though rarely encountered in the Loire and only occasionally in New Zealand, new-oak cooperage rears its ugly head incessantly in California. Don't even think about it!

Hard Cheeses

Examples: Parmigiano-Reggiano, American Asiago, aged Gouda, Vella Dry Jack, Spanish Roncal

If, like most people, you think of hard cheeses merely as a grated topping for "pisketty with tamayda sauce," a chunk of Parmigiano-Reggiano and a glass of thick, late-harvest **Amarone** from the Veneto will surely change your mind. Powerful, complex reds seem to become more mellow and elegant with these earthy, meltingly delicious, hard cheeses. **Barolo, Barbaresco** (both **Nebbiolo** wines from Piedmont), **Sangiovese**-based **Brunello di Mon-**

talcino, and even absurdly oaked, whorey "**Super Tuscans**" are perfect examples. Brawny **Châteauneuf du Pape** and other massive **Syrah/Grenache**–based beasts from the south of France, as well as young **Cabernet Sauvignon** from California, are also complemented in the same way. In other words, these are the cheeses for partnering colossal red wines that are simply too much for "normal" foods. Incongruously, these cheeses also make fantastic snacking alongside **Champagne** of every kind. Try that.

Blue-Veined

Examples: Stilton, Roquefort, Gorgonzola, Iowa Maytag Blue, Bleu de Gex, Spanish Cabrales

Salty and powerfully flavored, the blue-veined league of cheese has an affinity for one and only one style of wine: sweet. And the riper the cheese, the sweeter the wine. Fine Stilton and mature **port** make a regal combination of complex, mature flavors and textures at once complementing and contrasting each other. Roquefort and **Sauternes** is a sure thing. Delicate, crumbly Cabrales from Spain matches uncannily with dessert-grade sherries like **Creams**, sweet **Olorosos**, and **Pedro-Ximenez**. According to America's top cheesemonger, Steve Jenkins, Cabrales is "the only challenger to Roquefort for complexity of flavor, and a *must*-try." Gorgonzola *dolce* or, if you're lucky enough to find one, an aged Gorgonzola *(naturale)* can be sublime with a small glass of **poire William liqueur**! Try one of these cheese-wine combinations in place of dessert at your next meal.

Desserts

More and more I'm convinced that the concept of serving dessert wines alongside dessert is misguided at best. Yes, a lovely, peachy **Moscato d'Asti** and a peach tart are delicious together—but it's like putting whipped cream on ice cream. All we're doing is cranking up the sweetness and muddling the flavor of each.

Which brings me to my point. Dessert wines *are dessert!* These handmade, labor-intensive, small-production nectars are perfectly balanced and wholly satisfying on their own. A glass of sweet, decadent dessert wine sipped *before* espresso and a truffle is better for being a course unto itself.

If you insist on dessert wines with dessert, avoid chocolate and rich, cream-based desserts *unless there is a fruit element added*—for instance, a chocolate torte served with a raspberry coulis. In a pinch, I find a finger or two of strawberry jam, right out of the jar, will serve the same end: It adds an acidic element to the chocolate, which provides a bridge to the acidity in the wine. This said, I would still avoid squandering an expensive, complex dessert wine on such a blatantly sweet dessert.

These wines are much more interesting when paired with less sweet desserts like light custards and fruit pastries but are even better with cheeses, nuts, and fresh fruit. Try sliced nectarines with Beerenauslese **Riesling** or **Scheurebe,** toasted pecans with **Bual Madeira,** Roquefort with **Sauternes,** Stilton with **vintage port, Banyuls** or **Maury** (late-harvest **Grenache Noir)** from southern France's Roussillon, said to possess unique aphrodisiac powers.

Vin Santo, a late-harvest, partially oxidized, mysterious Tuscan dessert wine, is famous as the ultimate vinous accompaniment to "a leeeetle biscotti, you know." What's truly mysterious to me is what people see in a $40 or $50 dessert half-bottle that nine times out of ten is basically *not sweet!* (In Vin Santo's defense, I must add, when it's good, it's great.)

So . . .

Over the years, I've come to appreciate the exciting way the Old World's cuisines and wines must have naturally evolved together—classic regional dishes arose from local ingredients and were joined at the table by the wines that naturally flowered alongside them and became favored above all others. In modern America, however, access to countless ethnic foods, as well as a dizzying array of international wine choices, has created a bewildering number of possible combinations for which there are no "classic" wine touchstones.

My aim in this book has been to use the quantifiable aspects of a wine's acid/sugar balance and mouthfeel as a foundation for successful wine and food pairing. This concept should serve equally well when applied both to modern, cutting-edge cuisines and to more romantic, regionally specific ones.

Yet, I'm afraid it will take more than a little avenging to wean consumers from dull, oaky wines. My greatest hopes must reside in foodies everywhere to joyously serve up cool glasses of Riesling alongside their best culinary creations. Riesling from Germany is the single most flexible wine choice for today's foods. If you take away just one thing from my little book, I pray it's a new appreciation for the excellence and unparalleled versatility of Riesling.

Of course, if you want to take away a few other things, might I suggest the following:

- For a short course in wine/food pairing, I urge you to open multiple bottles at dinner whenever possible, comparing the wines of the food-friendly seven against any and all comers not on the list. In this way, you'll experience for yourself what drinks best with most foods.

- Be picky about your wineshop. Fine examples of the wines you seek will be difficult or impossible to find without a reliable, enlightened wine merchant. You may have warm feelings for your local mom-and-pop liquor store. That's nice. But unless said shop understands the principles addressed here, you'll be shortchanging yourself on quality for the sake of convenience.

- Resist wine brand advertising, label worship, and marketing. Become your own best wine authority.

P.S. In case there is anyone in the wine industry I haven't offended in this book, be patient. Simon & Schuster may really lose it and want more *Wine Avenger.*

In the meantime—wherever a retailer tries to slip a crummy wine into a customer's basket, I'll be there. Wherever there's a wine writer pandering to the masses, I'll be there. And wherever it is they put lunatics who rant about the most unpopular wine in the world as if it were the Second Coming, I'll be there. Come visit me. Please?

Index